BOND BEYOND BORDERS

Building Resilience, Navigating Cultural
Differences, And Cultivating
Lasting Relationship

SEBLE L. DESSALEGNE

Copyright © Seble Lemma Dessalegne, 2025

Bond Beyond Borders: Building Resilience, Navigating Cultural Differences, and Cultivating Lasting Relationships

All rights reserved
Except as permitted under the United States Copyright Act, no part of this book may be reproduced, stored in a retrieval system, or transmitted in any form or by any means — electronic, mechanical, photocopying, recording, or otherwise — without the prior written permission of the publisher, except for the use of brief quotations in a review.

ISBN Paperback: 979-8-9988347-1-4

First Edition
Book design by Turnedpagesco (turnedpagesco.com)
Published by Seble Dessalegne,
United States
+12026308069

For information about this book or to request permissions, please contact: @seblecreates or seble.lpetzoldt@gmail.com

Disclaimer

The advice provided in this publication is general in nature. It has been prepared without taking into account your individual life priorities, goals, financial or physical circumstances, or personal development needs. Before acting on this advice, you should consider its appropriateness with regard to your own capacity, objectives, and needs. To the maximum extent permitted by law, the author and the publisher disclaim all responsibility and liability to any person, arising directly or indirectly from any person taking or not acting based on the information in this publication.

ACKNOWLEDGMENT

This book would not have been possible without the experiences, communities, and individuals who have shaped my journey. I am profoundly grateful to my parents and every one of my family members for raising me with strong values, instilling a spirit of love, unity, and ambition, and encouraging me to always reach for higher aspirations.

To my husband, Oliver, for encouraging me to be brave, face my fears, and take action. His practical approach to life has helped me focus on what matters most: prioritizing logic and facts over emotion. To my daughters, Shania and Lillian, who've shown me that joy and connection need no words. Your love and energy have been a constant source of inspiration, comfort, and motivation, reminding me that no challenge is insurmountable.

To my father, Dr. Lemma Dessalegne, whose unwavering faith in my patience and determination has been a constant source of strength. His guidance and high standards have played a crucial role in shaping who I am today. To my mother, Tsedale Ayele, whose calming presence and uplifting spirit saw me through the toughest days. She nourished both my body and soul, allowing me to focus on my work while teaching me forgiveness, love, and respect for others, no matter the challenges they present. To my youngest sisters and brother, Bethlehem, Metadel, and Amanuel, your unwavering love, support, and dedication in uplifting me have kept me going.

ABOUT THE BOOK

Bond Beyond Borders serves as your essential guide to understanding people from different cultures and building meaningful connections across cultural divides. This book offers practical tools for nurturing cross-cultural relationships, raising children in multicultural environments, and navigating professional challenges in diverse settings. Whether you're living abroad, working in international or multicultural environments, or reconciling your personal identity with cross-cultural expectations, this book provides a clear path forward.

If you've ever felt out of place, torn between cultural norms, or exhausted from trying to fit in — you're not alone. Bond Beyond Borders empowers you to move beyond frustration and into transformation. Through deeply personal stories and accessible lessons, it shows how to shift your energy from seeking validation to cultivating resilience and inner peace. This book doesn't just teach cultural understanding — it helps you reclaim your happiness and build thriving relationships rooted in authenticity, compassion, and mutual respect.

TABLE OF CONTENTS

Acknowledgment iii
About the Book v

Introduction 1

1

NAVIGATING CULTURAL REALITIES 17
    Understanding Intercultural Relationships 17
    Small Aspects of Intercultural but Big Values 19
    Intercultural Travel 20
    The Subtle Moments of Turning Points 25
    Core Lesson 28

2

BREAKING FREE: NAVIGATING CHALLENGES,
SELF-ACCEPTANCE AND RELATIONSHIPS 29
    Don't try to convince anyone - Inform and
        Demonstrate 29
    The Feedback Trap to Fitting In 34
    Expecting Acceptance: A Sentence to Lifetime
        Struggle 38
    The Phases of The Relationship 40
    The Blueprint of Not Caring 46
    Understand the Reality We Live In 48
    Know What to Do Next 52
    Understanding You Need Grace and Love
        From Those in Your Life 56

Live Your Life, Honey!...56
Empower Yourself: Protect Your Inner Strength
  and Resources...61
Core Lesson...65

3
BUILDING A STRONG FOUNDATION:
PREPARATION, LEARNING, AND GROWTH 66
Readiness Matters – What's on the ground 66
Learn and Educate..69
Ready for What's Coming 72
Your Strength Develops—Give It Training and
  Time 76
Choose Your Battles 79
Core Lesson...83

4
FACING REALITY: CHALLENGES, TEMPTATIONS,
AND RESPECT IN RELATIONSHIPS...........................84
You are not extra special..84
Respect Your Partner..89
You Will Be Tempted to Give Up.............................99
Expect to Get Frustrated 102
Balancing Family, Culture, and Travel
  Frustrations...113
How National Perceptions Influence Your
  Actions..114
Core Lesson...130

5

EXPLORING NEW HORIZONS: THE ADVENTURES AND UNIQUENESS OF EXPERIENCES...................... 131
    Get Ready for the unique experience of a lifetime... 131
    Cheers to Never Being Boring! 135
    Viewing Tasks as an Adventure, Not a Burden... 137
    Core Lesson 143

6

THE JOURNEY OF YOUR CROSS-CULTURAL LOVE: LESSONS, STRUGGLES, AND STRENGTHS............ 144
    Navigating the Pros and Cons 144
    Design Your New Reality 148
    How to design your new norms............................. 149
    Confronting Prejudice: No Longer Ignorable........ 152
    Confronting Prejudice in Children.......................... 162
    The Importance of Learning and Teaching............ 165
    Helping Couples Navigate the Unique Dynamics 170
    Core Lesson 173

7

GUIDING PATHWAYS: EMPOWERING PARENTS, COMMUNITIES, AND SCHOOLS 174
    Empowering Parents to Support cross-cultural Couples and Mixed-Race Children.................... 174
    Mixed Couple Towards Their Parents 183
    Raising mixed kids 185

Unified Approaches to School Systems and
    Community Support Networks 189
Core Lesson 195

8

CRAFTING YOUR PATH TO VICTORY:
THE JOURNEY OF HEALING AND SELF-
DISCOVERY 196
    You Are Constantly Training for Victory 196
    The Victory and the Healing Process 202
    Let Go of the Victim Mentality and the Ego! 205
    There Is No "We" Until You Learn to Win
        Together 206
    The Power of Crafting & Building Your Own
        Path 207
    Core Lesson 221

9

FINAL TOUCH TO BREAKING STEREOTYPES
AND REINVENTING YOURSELF 222
    The Perception About That Country: Why It
        Matters 222
    Kill Old Version of You! Yes, That You! 226
    Core Lesson 230

10

THE PATH FORWARD: KEEPING LIFE EASY AND
ENJOYABLE 231
    Recognizing the Toughest Challenges and
        How to Overcome Them 231

Financial and Social Conflicts Management 240
Healthy Leaning In 243
The Mission Is Beyond You 247
Core Lesson 249

About the Author 250

INTRODUCTION

The intention of this book

In today's world, many things can feel triggering. With so much happening in the world, it often feels like our tolerance for differences is fading. Communicating without causing offense or navigating the reality that we're easily offended by others' words or actions has become an increasingly complex challenge. Building and maintaining cross-cultural, cross-country, and cross-social relationships can be tricky. Sometimes, it's because we don't know the "right" way to approach things, and other times, it's because we struggle to see the world from a wider, more inclusive perspective. When we encounter something unfamiliar, it often triggers an instinctive response. It feels foreign; it doesn't fit into our understanding of the world, and that discomfort can spark a fight-or-flight reaction. We may feel an urge to fight—to change others, to make them adopt our beliefs, values, or way of life. And when we can't, we may even feel the dangerous desire to destroy them. History is filled with tragic examples of how differences have led to conflict and violence, even to the point of genocide. People value their own principles over the dignity and lives of others.

On the flip side, we have the power to transform old perceptions into new ones and move beyond the layers of difference we've built that have caused us to lose the human connection we once shared—and continue to lose. What do we truly gain from emphasizing these differences? Instead, let's see how we all share the same humanity. How about we become lifelong students of one another, continuously learning and growing together in ways that transcend our borders and differences? Just like anything else in life, we can educate ourselves on how to embrace and bridge the gap. We can read books about the norms and values of other cultures and countries and pick up valuable insights from conversations with people from various backgrounds. A quick search online can open up a world of perspectives, helping us better understand how people from different parts of the globe perceive the world. We can also find ways to communicate with people from different races or countries in a respectful and meaningful way, even if it feels challenging at times. Gestures, tones, words, love languages, and expressions of respect or disrespect can have completely different meanings across cultures. It sounds simple, yet we often fail to put in the effort to truly understand these differences. This lack of understanding can lead to misunderstandings between colleagues, family members, friends, and even in-laws. The social aspect of our lives plays a huge role in our happiness, health, and success. The good news? We all could learn. By taking the time to understand and master how to engage with people from diverse cultural, social, and economic backgrounds, we can strengthen our relationships and create more meaningful connections.

The purpose of this book is to share the valuable lessons I've learned about developing communication skills in cross-cultural relationships, drawing from my personal experiences. Most importantly, it's about the insights gained through intercultural marriage and family establishments— cross-country connections that have emerged through international work, assignments, and studies abroad. The world's incidents and individual experiences have made us all more interconnected than ever before.

In the chapters ahead, we'll dive into what it truly means to be in intercultural relationships, the impacts they have, the challenges they present, and how you can navigate them. This book isn't meant to scare you or encourage hate; it's meant to inform you about the lessons that took me 20 years to learn and countless heartaches to figure out. Some of the challenges I discuss here, I handled with grace. However, others hit me so hard that it took days, if not weeks, to gather every ounce of strength just to keep going. In this book, I'll share how I trained myself, fought head-on, and ultimately overcame these challenges. And then there were moments when I simply smiled through the pain, realizing that sometimes, it's not worth fighting or that some people's ignorance is just too absurd to take seriously.

These are all lessons I never expected to learn, but life has taught me along the way. I didn't know what to expect, and much of the journey had me limping toward my goals, determined to fight for the future I envisioned, no matter the hurdles. Sometimes, I had the support of my family; other times, I had to face it all alone. Today, I'm here to share my story with you, hoping my experiences will inspire you to lift yourself up when life gets tough. This journey isn't always glamorous but requires being informed, resilient, and courageous enough to keep pushing forward.

How this book benefits you

Through years of extensive travel and living abroad, I have had the privilege of immersing myself in a variety of cultures and gaining a profound understanding of diverse ways of life, values, and traditions. This journey facilitated meaningful interactions with people from all walks of life, offering insight into how different societies approach communication, problem-solving, and daily routines. These experiences in varied settings have helped foster a rich tapestry of relationships and friendships, each shaped by unique perspectives and worldviews.

Spending time with families from different countries and becoming an integral part of their lives has been an enriching experience that taught me more than any textbook ever could. Whether sharing meals, embarking on adventures, or simply enjoying quality time together, these moments offered priceless insights into the daily routines, values, and traditions that shape each family's unique identity. Through these connections, I gained a broader appreciation for the world and a deeper understanding of the universal bonds that unite us all.

This book captures the essence of these experiences in navigating social and cultural relationships, as much as words can convey. As someone married to a white man and deeply rooted in traditional Ethiopian culture, I can confidently say that raising two children in such a diverse environment presents unique challenges, often more so than in typical relationships. Whether you believe this path was chosen by you or the universe, it's important to embrace the beautiful yet complex journey ahead. You deserve to fully embrace and enjoy the life that has been given to you.

To achieve this, we must learn how to navigate life without letting ourselves be easily triggered. But how can we do that? The key is developing effective communication skills and, most importantly, accepting ourselves and others as they are. The more we understand the world around us, the less stress we encounter. And with less stress, we can build more vibrant, flourishing connections and relationships.

It's important to approach this book with an open mindset, one that minimizes attachment to past events and instead views them as valuable lessons—tools for evaluating what serves us and what we can release. As someone from Ethiopia, I deeply appreciate our rich cultural and religious heritage, our central role in the African Union, and our long-standing tradition of hospitality. However, there are aspects of our social values that can sometimes hinder our openness to new ideas and prevent us from fully embracing others in our deeper spaces. These limitations can foster a work culture that stifles growth, contributing to economic insecurity and dependency.

This book is crafted to help you recognize both the challenges and the rewarding outcomes of understanding mixed-culture and cross-country relationships. It offers practical guidance on how to navigate and overcome these challenges, promoting a growth mindset that empowers you to rise to the demands of today's interconnected world.

While this book is particularly relevant for couples in interracial relationships, parents in mixed-culture relationships, children from diverse backgrounds, and those working in multicultural settings, it's also for educators, future leaders, and anyone committed to fostering global understanding.

The world is more interconnected than ever, and while it's easy to focus on our differences, the reality is that all nations and people, regardless of borders, are deeply intertwined. By acknowledging this interconnectedness, we can dismantle the barriers that divide us and work toward a more collaborative and prosperous future. One thing is clear: as the world continues to diversify, we will remain connected, no matter the physical borders we create.

I write this book with the hope that, even if I'm not your friend, family member, or partner, allow me to be a companion who has walked a similar path and can offer insights to help you avoid disappointments, prepare for challenges, and navigate your journey more effectively. Most importantly, I hope you take away at least one lesson that will guide you on this sometimes difficult journey we call life while also helping you embrace and enjoy your everyday experiences along the way.

In this book, I invite you to step outside your comfort zone for a moment. Open your heart to fresh perspectives and broaden your viewpoint with a genuine willingness to learn. Understand that we are all interconnected — whether through cross-border relationships, racial dynamics, or even tribal ties within the same region.

Glimpse into my life

On the final day of my swimming lesson certification during my sophomore year of high school, I fainted after completing the swimming test in the hot spring pool. I started losing consciousness before even leaving the water. I recall my classmates pulling me out, their faces a mix of shock and confusion. As I struggled to sit up, I looked up to see my mom's worried expression, her face a blend of concern and panic. I don't remember how they carried me to the washroom, where they frantically searched for cold water to cool my overheated body and face.

Our swimming teacher was from the UK, a kind man in his late 50s, and an exceptional sports and activities instructor. He organized excursions and trips for students during breaks between semesters. On the day of the trip, my mom was hesitant to let me go, especially since it involved swimming in a large pool without her supervision. She had always been afraid of letting me swim in deeper pools, and water and high diving terrified her.

On the other hand, my dad believed in the power of experience to teach life's most valuable lessons. He often said that if we kept our children in a comfortable bubble, they'd be unprepared when life inevitably presented challenges. Having lived in California, London, Tokyo, and Israel and traveled the world on his own, he understood the importance of allowing me to experience life independently.

Before I left, I tried to convince my mom of the value of teaching children independence and the importance of traveling from an early age. I reassured her by pointing out that there were plenty of teachers present, and she wouldn't be alone in her worries. With my persistent pleading, she eventually gave in.

Long story short, without informing anyone, she drove 25 kilometers to Sodere, a natural hot spring in Ethiopia, just to check on me. And that's exactly what happened.

As I slowly opened my eyes, I was relieved to see my mom standing by the bathroom, awake. I asked, "Mom, what are you doing here?" She replied, "I'm here, baby. This is exactly what I was afraid of. I didn't want to let you go." My only response was, "I'm okay, Mom. I passed. I got the certificate. I finished the laps," before lying back down.

She stayed with us the rest of the day, and we eventually went home. I believe we all realize that life holds beautiful moments, challenging moments, and unpredictable ones. But it's all contained within the safe home they've built for us. Children eventually step out of that safe zone, and the world lies beyond the walls of the home, beyond the town, the city, the country, and even beyond nations. There are things we can control and things we can't. Some experiences come to give us hope in the beauties of life, some to teach, and others to strengthen us.

Growing Up

After countless school trips, exams, incidents, and celebrations, I am at my grade 12 graduation ceremony. Standing proudly before my parents, feeling alive and grateful, I tell myself, "This is it. The happiest day of my life." I've earned good grades and become a decent person. Now, it's time for me to truly spread my wings. From there, I joined colleges and universities and pursued online studies — all in my quest to make myself proud and keep my parents even prouder.

Despite my strong stubbornness to follow my own path, my parents managed to keep me grounded, teaching me discipline and helping me grow into a professional young woman. As I worked and continued my studies, I began to understand more of what my father always said: "The world is beyond this house. Broaden your mindset; there are amazing things and challenges out there." And when I marveled at the beautiful nature in Ethiopia, he'd say, "Wait until you see the other stunning places in this world."

He always wanted me to aim higher and reminded me never to forget where I come from, no matter how far I go. "Always work hard, stay focused, and get to where you need to be," he would say. "But always keep your community, your country, and your nation in mind." They had a big vision for me, already visualizing where I could be and what I could accomplish with the patience I had.

With that guidance, I continued my work starting in 2003. In 2009, I joined international technology projects focused on integrating technology into education, economic growth, agriculture, and project mapping. These roles also took me to many beautiful places across Ethiopia. Through my work with NGOs and documentary film productions for health centers, I traveled extensively—from the Southern Nations to the Amhara, Oromia, and Tigray regions, training farmers, educating women, and visiting small local health centers.

Along the way, I learned so much about the diversity of landscapes, natural resources, lifestyles, cultures, and traditions. As the years went on, I had the opportunity to meet even more people from different backgrounds and countries.

As my mother would always say, "*Ayzosh, tichialesh fetari ale Kanchi gar,*" meaning, "Don't worry, you can do it. The Creator is with you." My father would remind me, "Keep going. With your patience, you'll achieve amazing things." "Remember, Life extends beyond our household—broaden your horizon." These wise words and the beautiful differences I've encountered along the way have constantly reminded me of the richness in our world.

Crossing Borders: How Travel Revealed the Similarities and Differences Between Cultures

Before I left Ethiopia in 2005, I saw the world through a very specific lens: our culture, our way of life, was the only "right" one, and Ethiopia itself was the most beautiful place on earth. Even though I interacted with people from different countries, I truly believed Ethiopia was the one true paradise, with the most stunning people and culture. To me, it was clear that everyone else must have been flocking to Ethiopia, as it was the epitome of beauty and authenticity.

Then, I moved to India, and everything changed. I was introduced to a whole new world of cultural perspectives, and I began to understand how people from different places viewed Africa and Africans in general. As an Ethiopian, I quickly realized I was met with a mix of expectations, assumptions, and even criticisms from people who couldn't even identify Ethiopia on a map. I'll never forget the curious stares, the comments like, "You look pretty—you look Indian now!" and the constant desire to touch my hair. These interactions sparked a deep curiosity in me about where these ideas came from. Eventually, I understood that these perceptions weren't rooted in malice but ignorance or a sheer lack of knowledge about Ethiopia's rich culture and history.

This pattern persisted as I journeyed to more countries. Over the past decade, I've had the chance to visit and live in places like Tanzania, South Africa, Pakistan, Germany, Italy, Switzerland, the Czech Republic, Spain, France, Romania, the USA, Albania, Mozambique, Thailand, Dubai, and Kenya to mention the least. But no matter where I went, the assumptions about me and my background remained the same. They simply morphed, adapting to the context of each new place. Along the way, I formed friendships with a diverse mix of people from all walks of life—intercultural couples from across the globe. I've met Spanish-Americans, German-South African couples, Mozambican-German pairs, Nigerian-German duos, Black American-Ethiopian relationships, Japanese-American-Black South African couples, and so on. Each encounter added another layer to my understanding of how our differences and assumptions about people shape our connections.

I've come to realize that we are all deeply connected across races and cultures. Life is so much bigger than the boundaries of our own communities, and as time passes, the world is moving toward more diverse societies. As humans, we often forget that we're all part of the same global family. We share so much in common, yet sometimes, we fail to remember that we are all made of the same blood and flesh.

Since becoming an adult, I've learned to see people for what they truly are — humans, first and foremost. My work has shown me the importance of treating everyone with respect, regardless of their race, culture, age, beliefs, religion, or financial situation. Over the years, I've witnessed how we all face similar medical and surgical challenges. We are all human, and we deal with the same struggles, share the same fears, and take pride in what we do. Our desires, dreams, and challenges are intricately woven together, yet we often fail to see how interconnected we truly are.

I didn't truly grasp this perspective until I left my home country and experienced it firsthand. While I had a theoretical understanding, I was sheltered by my comfortable environment and close-knit community, which limited my practical experience. But as I ventured out, I slowly began to see beyond our physical differences and recognize the deeper social dynamics at play. These dynamics shape our behavior and interactions for better or worse. The intercultural and psychological layers of how we relate to one another are often overlooked, yet they are essential to our well-being. Without this awareness, we tend to box people in, making assumptions about them before we've even had the chance to meet or connect.

When I returned from India in 2008, I began working in organizations that were diverse and multicultural, juggling roles as both a nurse and an IT professional in the US and European Projects. I had the incredible opportunity to collaborate with colleagues from all corners of the globe, each bringing their own unique perspectives. I even took a bold step and started my own company in South Africa. Coming from a small town with no prior experience in business or international relations, I found it challenging to overcome my shyness and the anxiety of interacting with people from such diverse cultures. Thankfully, thanks to my education-obsess, I had the knowledge and mastery of English I needed from a young age. I understood what was required in terms of work and communication, but I still found myself struggling to navigate what was considered appropriate or inappropriate in certain situations. I often worried about making mistakes or letting down my colleagues and bosses.

As I dove deeper into my work and pursued my master's degree, I discovered my world expanding, surrounded by diverse international professionals with varying socioeconomic backgrounds and leadership roles. Along with that expansion, my desires for the future began to shift. For many young women in the early 2000s, the path seemed straightforward. After completing your studies, date a well-educated Ethiopian man, get married, buy a house, have children, and live happily ever after. It was a familiar blueprint, but I realized that my journey might look different. That was the plan, at least. But after starting my first job after my MSc., I realized something pivotal: I wasn't ready to settle down. I saw an entire world of opportunities unfolding before me, and I knew I had the potential to accomplish so much more. So, in 2015, I made the bold decision to move to Pakistan. That moment marked a major turning point in my life, opening my eyes to a world of new experiences—both rewarding and challenging—that completely reshaped my perspective on what life could be.

Over time, though, I learned to embrace these challenges. I realized that mistakes were an inevitable part of the journey and that communication wasn't about being flawless; it was about learning, growing, and adapting as I went along.

Once I realized that all humans share similar fears, desires, challenges, and passions—whether related to people, things, or work—everything began to shift. This transformation became especially evident as I forged deep friendships and personal connections with people from Europe through my work. At the same time, I started to notice the stark contrasts between African, Asian, and European cultures in terms of family values, work ethics, personal boundaries, and even the unspoken rules of conversation. It was a journey of growth and self-discovery that expanded my understanding of others and helped me gain a deeper insight into myself and the world around me.

1

Navigating Cultural Realities

Understanding Intercultural Relationships

The real question is, how do you define an intercultural relationship? Some may even call it interracial, and others may say multicultural. You might hear someone describe you or your partner as coming from a "mixed family" or being a "mixed kid." Ultimately, it's quite simple: it's when two people from different countries or races come together in a marriage or relationship. No need to overcomplicate it. It refers to individuals from different cultural backgrounds, which can include people of the same or different races.

Now, race might come into play, but what do you call a relationship between, say, an African American and an Ethiopian or a Ghanaian and an Ethiopian? The core idea is simply that these are people from different countries. For the sake of simplicity, we'll focus on this straightforward definition.

As the book delves deeper in the coming chapters, you'll see that there are more complex issues that need to be addressed for these relationships to work—issues related to your relationship with your child, your parents, your in-laws, and your mixed and monocultural friends. For now, we're defining intercultural relationships in their simplest form to avoid unnecessary complexity, understanding that differences lie in backgrounds, family values, culture, religion, and social beliefs.

We won't dive into the political, social, economic, and technological factors that impact intercultural or interracial relationships just yet. The truth is, even within European relationships—like Swiss-German and so on—there are still challenges. The same holds true within Asian relationships, whether it's Japanese-Chinese, Korean-Indian, or Korean-Japanese. There are always factors that contribute to the emergence of prejudice in relationships. The same applies to mixed African couples. For instance, a South African married to a Nigerian may encounter similar challenges stemming from the assumed socioeconomic factors that exist between their culture. So, what is an intercultural relationship? Simply put, it's a relationship between two people from different countries.

Small Aspects of Intercultural but Big Values

When you think of a country, you might think of its language, appearance, food, clothing, traditions, norms, values, beliefs, artifacts, symbols, and more. What may seem small or insignificant to you could be incredibly important to someone else. For example, how you cook chicken might feel trivial, but when someone prepares it for you in the traditional way you're familiar with, it can hold significant meaning. Similarly, what you do, how you do it, and when you do it can carry vastly different significance for various individuals.

Growing up, each of us is shaped by the culture of our family and our country. When you encounter someone from a different cultural background, it's natural to wonder how they perceive the world and approach life differently from you. Let alone when it occurs between individuals from two different countries. There are those from the same country but geographically from different sides. One can be from the East and the other from the West, bringing in different cultures from both ends when they unite in marriage or other relationships; thus, even though there's that common understanding of being from the same country, they still have different values and ways of things in the society. In all these scenarios discussed so far, it is important to avoid disregarding one's culture to create the unity and bond needed. That's why it's crucial to understand at least some key aspects of cultural diversity to minimize ignorance of others' cultures with a worldview that goes beyond geographical locations and borders.

Intercultural Travel

Before we start categorizing things, let me share some real, on-the-ground experiences of the two main cultures we'll explore—Ethiopian and German cultures, to name just a few of the countries discussed here. I know it's impossible to fully capture the essence of any country in words, let alone explain everything in one piece of writing. It's not easy to help others truly understand how things are or how they feel unless you've lived there and been part of the community. That said, I can offer a brief overview. Here it is, in a nutshell.

The Ethiopian culture is very family- and community-oriented, which means not only in the literal social aspect of living but also in practical ways. Insurance, therapy, and financial security are heavily reliant on social networks. Getting things done, like finding a job or receiving physical assistance for any kind of disability, is not typically funded by formal systems but rather by the community. By "social," means family, neighbors, or community groups, such as church or mosque members. Family relations are highly important. Without asking, there will always be someone to help you with something or pitch in advice on handling your situation.

Being born and raised in Ethiopia means you are part of that community, like the neighborhood child. The entire neighborhood feels like one big family; if you love having a large community that is there with you all the time, you will love it! Then you have close-knit communities, with groups of mums and dads who would support one another through both tough times and joyful moments. Fathers were highly respected for their status and age, while working mothers often organized large family gatherings and events from time to time. Mom, always dressed in her classy outfits, with sunglasses on and driving like a SuperSport competition fast or furious game. You see strong African women in practice. Working as an accountant during the day, an excellent mother and wife to her husband by the evening, and a big event organizer on the weekends. Community gatherings were frequent, ranging from large barbecue-style events to simpler ones with light snacks, where people would share traditional Ethiopian bread *(difo dabo)* and *kolo* (a wheat-based Ethiopian snack). If someone were short of an egg for breakfast, you'd simply borrow one or two from your neighbor. It was a beautiful, simple way of life centered around community and connection.

Back then, human connections were genuine, with no interference from social media. There were no mobile phones at the dinner table when everyone shared stories about how their day went. Presenting the books you read like you're hosting your own personal book club because, apparently, after-school family time wasn't complete without a little literary analysis. Card games and chess provided hours of fun with uncles. Computers were simply on desks, where they belonged, and in our spare time, we spent it gardening or checking on the 40 chickens in the backyard to see if they'd laid eggs for breakfast.

Trips with your mother to get milk for breakfast were moments to treasure. All the food was homemade, organic, and made with love by your aunties or your mom. If you need help, all you have to do is call on one of your nannies, who has been there since you were little. The house was always bustling with people, even when your parents were at work. There was always someone around to cook, take care of the children, and manage the household. Grandmothers and mothers never had to worry about a thing.

Family gatherings were frequent, with buffet-style meals and relatives coming from different towns, often with their children to stay over. It is so much fun for children growing up with memories to cherish. It was a truly community-based system.

Now, let's turn to Western culture. The system is highly independent. Children are raised to be strong and prepared to face the world, assuming they have only themselves and the government to rely on for success. Family relationships are important, and while they will help if you ask, the support is often limited to what's necessary until you can get back on your feet. This fosters a sense of individuality, allowing people to pursue their own paths with minimal expectations from others.

In the 1970s, working part-time was particularly encouraged for mothers, allowing them to have more family time. This schedule enabled them to come home earlier and fulfill social expectations, helping maintain family dynamics as the country transitioned into a high workforce culture. Although it wasn't as vibrant as the social life in the African context, there was more time for socializing and connecting with family and friends back then compared to today.

In Germany, no external person is overly concerned with how you manage your finances or your life. All responsibilities fall on you to handle your things yourself. If you make mistakes, you bear the consequences yourself—no one else is responsible for your choices. You mind your own business, and you don't get involved in someone else's issues. Ultimately, you are expected to be self-reliant.

In general, German culture has less tolerance for weakness, mistakes, unpreparedness, or misbehavior in contrast to Ethiopia. Concepts like time management, the significance of appointments, and the approach to addressing issues—directly in Germany and indirectly in Ethiopia—give communication different meanings in each cont.

Thus, your relationships, career, finances, personal goals, parenting, religious beliefs, and social decisions are influenced by these factors from both perspectives. Living differently or according to your own values will require you to make your own choices based on the experiences that have shaped you from birth to today. Achieving your goals and living your fullest life involves sacrifices on certain cultural expectations, making different commitments, ongoing decision-making, and the effort to make the right choices along the way. This is true whether you are navigating intercultural relationships, seeking success, or striving to be a better parent.

Now, imagine traveling to either of these two countries as an African, and then try to put yourself in the shoes of a European living in both of these scenarios. Coming from a mixed family with so many differences presents its own set of challenges, such as figuring out where and how to fit in. In African societies, which are often tightly knit, even slight deviations from the norm can make it hard for others to recognize your place within the society. As a result, you may receive little to no support, as you can be perceived as an outsider. The same can happen in reverse.

This isn't because either group consists of bad people, but rather because human nature tends to react to foreign people and behaviors like our bodies react to foreign substances, in fight or flight. So, humans' first instinct would be to fight the new or flight away when something or someone unfamiliar feels like a threat. Anytime you travel to a new place or move to another country, trying to integrate into the community can sometimes make you feel like an outsider. Initially, there's often rejection until both learn, adapt, and begin to live together in harmony.

The Subtle Moments of Turning Points

There's an Ethiopian saying, *wuhha siwesd eyasasake new*, which means, "You're swimming and enjoying the water, but without realizing it, the water is carrying you somewhere you never intended to go." Life can be like that. The current might take you to beautiful experiences and destinations you never imagined there would be. Or it could lead you to tough challenges that feel hard to swim through and take you to unexpected places. But if you keep swimming with the effort you have in you, keep making the turns that are right for you, trust, and know that, in the end, everything will be okay.

At times in life, you start out just swimming for fun, and before you know it, you're swimming every day. Eventually, you learn to surf, and you might even swim across to a new place, a richer side of life. Before you realize it, you're exactly where you need to be. Much like other parts of our journey, one move is like a stepping stone to the next destination.

The same applies to intercultural relationships, whether in the workplace, marriages, or family dynamics. Cultural differences can create challenges, especially when couples come from diverse backgrounds. Children can feel confused about communication styles and cultural norms, adding complexity to family dynamics.

Turning points in life can be confusing and scary at times, but it might be one of the best things that have happened to you, only to realize once years have passed and you have gone through the challenges and made it through. Now, before going deeper, let's see those turning points that are leading to cross-cultured relationships.

For some, it is the desire to pursue further education and better opportunities. Many go overseas to enhance their skills and credentials, believing it will open new doors for them. For some, the journey abroad is temporary—returning home to contribute to their communities in meaningful ways. For others, the experience abroad extends into long-term stays, where they build new careers, forge relationships, and even settle down. Some may find love, get married, and start families in a foreign land, then start learning the values and norms and understanding the cultures and traditions of each other, ultimately filling in the gaps between the two differences and becoming one.

For others, it is the world travel desires that bring cross-cultural relationships. Many young people, especially after finishing high school or fulfilling citizenship duties, take time off, often six months to a year, to figure out what they want to do with their lives. It's become increasingly common for parents to save money specifically to support their child's travel during this period, allowing them to explore the world before committing to studies, a career, or relationships.

In other cases, individuals may work intensively for a few years, only to feel burnt out. They then decide to take a break, disconnect from their routine, and travel for an extended period to recharge and reflect. For some, this break turns into something longer as they realize they want to pursue a different direction in life.

Regardless of the reasons behind the travel, these journeys often lead to new encounters with people. Some may meet a partner and enter into a committed relationship, while others might start new ventures, such as opening a restaurant or joining a company.

Before you know it, you're surrounded by intercultural and international connections. Now, it's time to learn how to navigate these new dynamics. Whether it's the job you're passionate about, the beautiful person you've met, or the charming individual you've fallen in love with, these experiences will shape your life. To make it all work, effective communication—both with the people around you and with those who are important to them—becomes crucial.

For some individuals, it is the involvement in national programs like job creation and business development in developing countries or starting new business partnerships in a new country. This leads to adopting the new food and cultures, making new good friends, and possibly falling in love.

Then comes the journey of dating, marriage, and having kids. You meet someone who catches your eye, and that connection grows into a relationship over time. Months turn into years, and eventually, you're married.

Now, as a mixed couple in a multicultural environment, you must learn how to navigate life in this new dynamic. The union brings children and, with that, the responsibility to raise them in the best way possible, blending and honoring both cultures in their upbringing.

As you continue to pursue your dreams and enjoy the beauty of these experiences, challenges start to emerge. One of the most significant things is misunderstood communications and misconceptions in general. And then there's the personal ones. The sad holidays are because of missing things that are dear to your comfort and joy—lacking from important cultural and family occasions. With one family on one side of the world and the other on the other, travel restrictions—like visa issues and paperwork—can make visiting difficult. This creates a sense of disconnect, preventing you and your partner from fulfilling your social duties and impacting your parents, extended families, and even your children, who are deprived of essential familial bonds and experiences.

Core Lesson

Culture shapes how we love, travel, and connect—embracing differences opens the door to deeper relationships.

2

Breaking Free: Navigating Challenges, Self-Acceptance and Relationships

Don't try to convince anyone - Inform and Demonstrate

One evening, you find yourself at a cocktail event after a conference, mingling with a diverse group of people from various African and European countries. You would be the only Ethiopian in the circle, and you would find yourself discussing website designs and user-friendly interfaces for African educators and students. Suddenly, one person in the group said, "Ethiopians can't design at all," dismissing the idea that there was any point in discussing it with Ethiopians. You would remain quiet at first, but then you feel compelled to point out that there are, in fact, some excellent professionals in Ethiopia. Trying to convince them, but as this person continued to belittle designers from Ethiopia, the others looked increasingly confused, and it became clear that he had already made up his mind—nothing you say could change it.

Years pass by, and you meet more people and have more conversations. You realize that everyone seems to be trying to convince someone of something based on their own experiences or justify why one person or group is more valuable. One person may need to be paid well while another does not. One deserves respect, while another does not. One is assumed to be smarter and more civilized in their behavior, while the other is not. It's a constant battle over who is worth more. It is true that skills can vary on an individual basis and are influenced by exposure, but your passport or where you come from shouldn't generally dictate how you are treated or accepted in the workplace or personal relationships.

On another occasion, in a beautiful, vibrant place in Hamburg, Germany, everyone was in a good mood and gathered to celebrate the upcoming new year. Suddenly, the same conversation you had heard before began to rise. You would think, not this again, feeling so fed up with it. Then, questions begin to be raised to get to know each other a bit. "Where are you from?" And "What do you do for a living?" and all. As an African woman with a white partner, people often expect to hear a certain story: "I met him in a club, we hooked up, and now we're here," or "You're that trophy girl a white guy can show off to his friends to prove he's not racist." Sometimes, they frame it as "She's this beautiful black girl who needed a white man to rescue her from her miserable life." No one anticipates a story of love at first sight, meeting at work, or connecting through mutual friends.

When you have lived long enough in an intercultural community, you learn how to answer these questions. However, initially, people from low-income countries would try to explain that she/he is not just a poor girl/boy who had been picked up from the street, detailing how they met while working on the same tech company and implementation project. He would mention that her father is a remunerated doctor and researcher, and he has written multiple books that you would find around the globe, including in the Dresden Public Library. And it goes on to say that her mother is a business owner and accountant. He would describe how my siblings are crushing in health tech and live comfortably in the U.S. with their families. You'd get drained from constantly explaining yourself, justifying, and trying to make others feel comfortable, all at the expense of your own well-being. But you understand the point: in interracial relationships or intercultural settings, especially if you come from a less fortunate background, there is often a desire to convince others of your worth.

As someone from a different culture, you may feel the need to explain your partner's background to help others understand and respect them equally and, hopefully, appreciate them the way you do. You might find yourself trying to clarify that Germans aren't rude; they're just more direct, which can sometimes be off-putting. Or, as an Irish person, you might have to explain why you feel the need to speak before leaving a room. As an Ethiopian, you could be justifying why you eat with your hands, even at restaurants. You might explain why your husband prefers to leave family gatherings after an hour or why he doesn't want visitors when your baby is only a few months old. All of this explanation is just to help you and your partner be accepted. But in the end, it often feels like a waste of time. Later in this book, a completely different approach will be suggested—one that promotes a more peaceful and less draining one.

As a young person, you probably don't fully realize the amount of work this entails. You don't truly understand it until you move out of your family's home and start facing life on your own, with no one around to guide you on what to do or what to avoid. You grow up, become an adult, and start meeting all kinds of people—some who accept you and others who don't. Some will like you, while others might just hate you. You find yourself constantly explaining who you are to everyone.

And then, you start dating, get engaged, and marry someone outside your tribe. Suddenly, the life you once imagined becomes even more complicated. You're now exposed to all kinds of people, each with their own views and opinions. People want to assess your intentions and abilities. Relationships can vary, but your reasons for being in them can differ drastically. For example, one nurse might work in the field simply to pay the bills, while another does it with a genuine passion for saving lives.

No matter the type of job you take or the reasons behind it, the goal is to convince your employer that you're passionate about the work. In reality, you're likely after the job because it helps advance your career, supports your family, or allows you to achieve the lifestyle you want. A potential employer hires you because they believe you can do the job. Once you're in the role, there's no need to constantly prove yourself; just focus on doing the job you're already skilled at. You don't have to go to your boss every day and remind them of your abilities.

The same applies to relationships. Once you've committed to your partner and accepted them for who they are, there's no need to justify your choice every day. Constantly defending your relationship can be draining, especially for couples who feel the need to explain their decisions. You might consider yourself someone who doesn't care about others' opinions, or you might be more of a people-pleaser. Either way, you often find yourself doing things for others or to fulfill a specific expectation. It feels rewarding when someone appreciates you, but if your peace depends on those approvals, you're heading for an unhappy life. At some point, we all try to convince others that we're making the right choices. And, let's be honest, for every new thing you bring into your community, the first reaction you'll often get is, "But why?" And they will never be convinced or be sure of your life choices as you do. So stop trying and do your thing. Live your life.

You don't owe anyone an explanation for why your partner is good enough for you. If you know the truth about your relationship and who you are, that should be enough. But there's more to it. Others may never fully understand, and that's okay. In this book, we'll explore how to find joy in the work of relationships, trust your instincts, and live life on your own terms. Whether your decisions are good or bad, you'll be the one to live with the consequences. No one else will be there to experience it for you — to share in the joy, face the challenges, or help you pick yourself back up. This life is going to be a tough journey. The topics we explore from here on will open your eyes to where you need to accept things, where you should stand firm, and what you need to let go of. You will learn where to build and which corners to ignore so you can live a happy, free, and joyous life. So, get cozy, grab your snack, and let's dive in.

The Feedback Trap to Fitting In

When you are young, it's important for you to seek your parents' love and approval and to make sure your parents are never disappointed — always looking forward to making your loved ones proud. To put the picture for you. In this case, you, let's say you have this amazing father who is a renominated doctor and researcher, highly disciplined, and the most humble guy you know on this planet. You have a mother with so much strength, resilience, and professionalism, always dressed on point, and a classy boss lady who runs her own two businesses: the most resilient woman and a dedicated prayer mother. And you, as a child, would be thriving to come to their high standards of performance, being respected, classy, and one of the top performers and you eventually do well for yourself.

Then you grow up, see things from a different perspective away from home, and life becomes real. You see how they made it look simple while it is harder than it looks. Some part of you wants to do what makes you happy. Some parts of you want to live for their approval or acceptance of what you do. If you grow up in a country like Ethiopia, you know that this means full time thriving. It means everyone who thinks they helped raise you in the neighborhood has an opinion on your life. Everyone has a suggestion about how you need to dress, act, and do things as a girl, how you should study and when to study, who to date, whom to hang out with, what career you should follow, whether you should buy a house or a car, how you should take care of your child, what to do for your face care and so on. It's endless and destructive at times. If you allow it, they will be running the affairs of your life, not you. So, you need to be mindful of who is running your life; otherwise, you end up being trapped in that endless loop of fulfilling their expectations. Waiting for their good approval to be accepted and eventually, you are trapped in that hell-like prison of recognition instead of living the life you dream of living. In the end, it might not even be good enough for them.

Since it's deep in your upbringing, you sometimes find yourself constantly seeking validation—wanting to hear "well done" or "you're doing great." They'll offer praise only when it aligns with their views, giving you that boost for your ego, much like a drug. There will be days when you feel in your gut that you're doing the right thing, yet they respond with "umm, that's not good" or give you disapproving looks. Before long, everything revolves around their feedback, trapping you in a cycle of needing recognition from your loved ones. The same goes for acceptance among friends and when you try fitting in a community instead of being you. When you propose something new and outside the box, it often gets a firm "no" until they eventually come around, which can take years until they have their "aha" moment.

How many years and rounds of justification will you endure before you can truly live life on your own terms? The truth is, every child—because, in their eyes, we never truly outgrow that role—seeks approval from their family. They try to guide us in the best way they know, driven by love and concern. But this can create a dependency that feels restrictive. Pretending to accept their guidance without addressing it leads to resentment over time. Learning how to communicate effectively, turning down certain ideas, and setting boundaries will become necessary. You'll need to discern which advice to embrace and which to graciously decline with love.

Then there's the support you seek from your partner. You want your partner to understand you. If you're a woman, you desire affection and want to be treated with respect and appreciation like a queen at times. The little boy in your partner needs to feel that he is providing for and protecting you as a man. You both want to be respected, listened to, loved—the list continues. In both scenarios, if you both aim to receive this every time you take action, you risk getting trapped in that same loop, constantly seeking their reactions and feedback. While you both need support at times, it shouldn't be a constant requirement. Sometimes, there needs to be a silent trust, where you both understand and appreciate each other's efforts and sacrifices without always putting it into words. You know he values what you do, and he knows how much you cherish him as a provider and the love you share. You know you're special. You know you're a good-looking, strong, and handsome man. Whatever qualities you recognize in yourself, embrace them and find happiness in them. Only then can you offer the love your partner truly needs. If you can't find happiness within yourself as an individual, it will be difficult to be happy together as a couple. Isn't that freeing? Free yourself from the need for your partner's constant approval and validation to feel confident in your choices. Likewise, allow your partner the freedom to do the same.

The key is to break free from that cycle—the trap of constantly seeking feedback. It's perfectly okay to turn down input from family and friends. But don't misinterpret this: some of their feedback or reactions may carry valuable wisdom and be genuinely helpful. The real skill lies in being able to assess which insights are relevant to you, based on their experiences, and what makes sense for your situation. It's important to know where to set boundaries and how to communicate them effectively. As you dive into this book, you'll discover how to navigate life in a smarter way rather than learning the hard way.

Expecting Acceptance: A Sentence to Lifetime Struggle

One thing we can all agree on is that we all want to be accepted for who we are, no matter where we go. However, that's not always easy. Finding a sense of belonging can be challenging in a society full of differences, especially if you come from a different country or cultural background. Even if you're just living your life within your own community, you might notice that people often seem tense, as if they're ready to be offended.

We've hardened our hearts, refusing to accept anything that even slightly challenges our views. Past betrayals and losses have fueled this intolerance. It's rare to encounter people who are open to new ideas and welcoming of newcomers. Tolerance for our differences has decreased to the point where we may wish harm upon each other—whether through actions or words. It's becoming increasingly difficult to find people who accept you for who you truly are, especially among those you value, respect, and love.

What happens if they don't accept you? To make matters worse, what if all you face is rejection? At times, you may be labeled the troublemaker, the thief, the loud one, or the source of drama. Sometimes, the generous one and then the stingy one. You might even be seen as someone who creates distance between people or who disrespects or dislikes other cultures. To add another layer of challenge, you're in a relationship with someone not only from a different part of the world but from a different race. At one point, you were part of your original community, but suddenly, you no longer belong because you've introduced someone new into the mix. As your relationship progresses, being a mixed couple can make going to certain places increasingly difficult to enjoy. You visit either of your two countries, and neither seems sure how to accept you. You may find yourself thinking, "These are my friends, my family—how can they not understand?" You try to explain, "Hey, it's me—your friend, your son/daughter," yet still feel misunderstood. They might think you've changed, but the truth is, you haven't just evolved. Certain things about you have changed. Of course, everyone evolves, and the fact is that unity and understanding will return in time only if both sides are willing to accept this. Relationships must go through certain phases before reaching the acceptance point. Be prepared, as it's a journey that begins with excitement and ends with unshakable love. Keep reading to discover how this process unfolds.

The Phases of The Relationship

As humans, we go through various stages in life, each affecting us in different ways. From infancy to childhood, adolescence, adulthood, and eventually old age, we experience distinct developmental phases. These stages encompass mental, emotional, and physical growth, each influencing our overall well-being. The same process applies to loss. These stages continue to be widely used today to help individuals understand and navigate their emotions as they heal through grief.

When coping with grief, we typically go through five stages, known as DABDA (Denial, Anger, Bargaining, Depression, Acceptance) as the model introduced by Elisabeth Kübler-Ross in her 1969 book On Death and Dying.

Similarly, your intercultural relationship goes through phases, starting from the moment you meet your new partner to the development of an unshakable bond that extends not only between the two of you but also to your in-laws and those around you.

The Excitement Phase

In this stage, everyone, including you, is filled with excitement. This is something new—like buying a shiny pair of fancy shoes that you can't wait to wear. Or, if you are into fancy cars, you are buying that dream car and can't wait to take it for a ride. You want to experience how it feels and show them off to your loved ones and friends. You constantly talk about it. You can't wait to constantly take care of it. In the same way, a new relationship is exciting. Especially when you meet the man or woman of your dreams, it's exciting. You can't take your hands off each other. You pick her up early, so you can't wait to spend time with her or him. You check your phone every minute to see if he has texted or called. Like with everything else that brings you joy, you decide to share it with others. After a while, you're eager to introduce them to your friends and family. It's all fun and exciting.

The Curiosity Phase

Now, curiosity takes over, leading to a flurry of questions: "Is it getting serious?" "What's it like to have a relationship with a foreigner?" People bring their stereotypes into the conversation. For example, they might ask, "So, how is she? If she's African, does he spoil you? If it's a white guy, have you met his family yet? Or if he's from Japan, you must be having sushi for breakfast, right?" If he is from Germany, it was often, "So, how is it being with a German guy? Oh wow, that sounds tough. Aren't they racist?" Making you feel as if you are living with a version of Hitler. If South African, the assumed question of him being a gangster or some kind of criminal. These comments often come from people you love and respect, which can create confusion about the person you're learning to love. As a result, you may start to doubt, and that doubt leads to questioning your partner, marking the transition into the next phase. If you're not grounded enough in this turbulent journey, you risk breaking each other's hearts, possibly leading to a breakup.

The Battle Phase

This phase is all about conflict! Everyone seems to be fighting with someone else. You find yourself arguing with your partner, family, and vice versa. Misunderstandings abound: "Oh, I didn't mean it that way," "My mum didn't mean to say you're dumb," "My sister is just like that," or "He doesn't dislike your cooking; he just doesn't eat pork." "No, I didn't mean you look ugly; I just don't like extensions." "You must be after my money," "You must have thought I was easy because I am African," on and on. These arguments often stem from misunderstandings that don't even pertain to the couple. The conflicts lead to frustration and resentment if you're not careful.

Here's a simple example: A 70-year-old Swiss mother-in-law might show her son's wife, who is from Ghana, how to use the microwave. As an African, you might wonder why she feels the need to demonstrate this, questioning if she thinks you can't figure it out. This can quickly feel offensive. Instead of addressing her directly, you go to your Swiss husband and complain about his mother. As you can imagine, this could derail the family gathering and potentially turn into a full-blown argument. The cycle continues on his side too—he might share negative stereotypes about her country of origin, and the next argument could escalate into something like, "You didn't clean up," implying it's your fault just because you're African. This is often rooted in generalizations, such as the misconception that Africa is dirty and that trash is thrown around carelessly. In this dynamic, even seemingly small things, like eating pork—which is common in many European and Western dishes—can become highly sensitive topics.

Imagine a medieval battlefield where everyone is swinging swords and shooting arrows, unsure of who they're fighting for. This chaotic communication mirrors many intercultural relationships. If your family bond isn't strong and your relationship feels fragile, you won't survive this phase. You're emotionally drained, leading to giving up and resulting in a return to singlehood.

The Surrender Phase

At this point, you both feel exhausted and might find yourselves on the couch saying, "Uffey!" in the Ethiopian way, "Shade!" in the German way, or "Shame!" in South African slang. Just like you, your loved ones are also emotionally exhausted. Everyone is wounded, and it's essential to take a break to heal those wounds. This pause is necessary! Trying to correct mistakes through conversation could lead to further harm. Give everyone, including you and your partner, time to heal and learn about each other's differences and common things.

The Acceptance Phase

By now, your family and friends will start to accept that you're in a relationship outside your tribe. They may struggle to accept your differences, but you'll feel a measure of acceptance for the choices you've made. Still, something may feel uncomfortable each time you meet them. You used to be one of them, and while you still are, you're also now an outsider. They may choose their words carefully around you, and you might find yourself second-guessing what you say to avoid reopening old wounds.

The Learning Phase

After cycling through various phases, you begin to step back and learn about your partner's culture and individual background. Instead of questioning why they don't understand or do things the way you believe is right, you start to appreciate their upbringing and the values that govern their country. Through conversations, books, documentaries, spending time with locals, and gradually immersing yourself in the culture, you start to understand why things are the way they are and how they function in that country. At this stage, your relatives and friends also begin to learn and gain insight into the different ways of doing things and the cultural differences shaped by diverse upbringings and values between the two races. The realization that the world extends beyond your own community, combined with a desire to make the relationship work, sparks curiosity and encourages a deeper awareness of the cultural backgrounds of others.

Over time, this gradual accumulation of knowledge builds, deepening your understanding day by day and year by year.

The Unshakable Love Phase

After months, possibly years, of navigating ups and downs, you arrive at a place of strong, exciting love. Your relationship feels lively and fresh every time, and your loved ones and community begin to accept you as part of the family. Sometimes, it may even feel like they respect and accept you more. You might feel more excitement and appreciation directed towards you than your local partner. For instance, in some European families, members and friends may seem more eager to embrace your African partner, offering more care and attention than they would to your European partner. Meanwhile, your European partner might receive more love and attention in Africa than they do back home. It sounds a bit ironic, right? But strangely, it works out quite well.

The whole point here is that you are learning to understand that you will never fully return to your old tribe as one of them. You will never fit in, but you created your new. Your new tribe. Your new family. Your new partner becomes your family. For real, you practically leave your parents to unite with your spouse, and this truth becomes more evident when you marry. As you start a family, your children and partner become your true home. Throughout these phases of life, the universe guides you to let go of past attachments and focus on building connections where you are now and where you need to be.

The earlier you accept that you will never fit in completely, the happier you will be. The moral here is to stop seeking acceptance and instead focus on your growth and evolution. If you choose to chase approval endlessly, you'll find yourself in a never-ending battle with no clear winner. This emotional and mental exhaustion can lead to feelings of confinement, making you feel as though you have to constantly prove and explain yourself, which is physically draining and ultimately unhappiness-inducing for both you and your loved ones.

So, free yourself from the start and avoid heartbreak. Understand the process and be prepared as you navigate through these phases.

The Blueprint of Not Caring

Now, let's break it down and dive deeper. If you begin this journey believing that love from your family or partner is unconditional, you're setting yourself up for disappointment. However, if you receive genuine acceptance, especially from those who matter most to you, that's wonderful! But it's important to also prepare yourself for the possibility that it may not happen. In that case, you should be able to be at peace with who you are or the choices you are making. To help with this, here are a few things you'll need to practice.

First, Know Where Your Energy Lies

In life, there are things and people we deeply care about, those we care about only halfway, and those we don't care about at all. Sometimes, we get carried away by situations and end up investing our energy and time in things that are irrelevant to our personal and family lives. Eventually, we realize that it's not important to care about them at all.

We often intertwine our self-worth with what others think of us. Some of us even prioritize everyone else's happiness over our own comfort, carrying the burden of their joy instead of our own. We often worry about whether others like us or not. Here's a fun fact: people are generally more focused on themselves than you. The truth is, some people are only in your life temporarily, and their affection can fade the moment you say something they disagree with. We sacrifice so much of our own happiness just to ensure they approve of what we do or say. So, why do we feel the need to convince others to like us? Why do we seek their understanding? The reality is that they're already busy trying to understand themselves. Everyone craves understanding, which leads to a situation where everyone tries to convince others of their own viewpoints. The ironic truth is that we all have people and things that truly don't matter to us, no matter how much someone tries to convince us otherwise — and that's perfectly okay.

The Moral of the Story

Free yourself from the chains of trying to make others understand your choices. Avoid expecting unconditional love and support, as it's something that doesn't truly exist. Stop pouring your energy into convincing people that this is what you want. After all the explanations and sacrifices you've made, they may still not understand. Occasionally, they might make an effort to understand a bit, but often, it turns out they were just nodding along to smooth over the conversation. There are countless examples that people and you experience on a daily basis. This applies equally to the relationship choices you make for yourself.

Your primary focus should be on those who genuinely matter to you, and that starts with you.

If you don't care about rugby, then don't waste your energy trying to convince rugby fans that football is better. If a colleague you don't particularly like is leaving, and the office committee asks you to contribute $5 for a farewell party you are not interested in attending, don't do it. Forcing yourself to care about things that don't resonate with you only adds stress and consumes your joy. If you want to live a happy life, especially in intercultural situations, you need to free yourself, one step at a time.

Understand the Reality We Live In

Let's say there are times when you sit with some family members or friends and discuss exercise and health issues you've observed in the hospital because you're deeply invested in these topics. After a while, they would change the subject or excuse themselves to the kitchen or bathroom. It would be different if you were sitting with a physician, nurse, or anyone interested in the science behind it all. Similarly, just as you have no interest in politics, you can't expect them to care about your passions. We all choose what to care about, and we certainly can't invest ourselves in everything. So, stop pouring your energy into things that don't matter. It might sound harsh, but it's a choice you need to make—deciding what to compromise on and what to prioritize—judge where the balance lies for your own inner satisfaction. Listen to your heart and trust your instincts in your decisions. The truth is that everyone is primarily invested in themselves. Focus on yourself and stop worrying too much about others.

While it may take some time for certain individuals, for others, it comes easily and naturally. Master the art of not caring. What does that mean? Why are we even discussing this? This is why. Just like anything else, the same fact applies to relationships. And relationships are challenging. Moreover, interracial relationships do feel like more of a mission than a mellow life. Such relationships often require more effort than those within the same culture.

When you start dating someone outside of your race, you face comments, insults, suggestions, and predictions from others about who you will become as individuals and as a couple. It can feel like a bad dream. If you let it, this scrutiny can break you. You may start to doubt yourself.

You start asking yourself, "Am I making the right choice?" "Am I really the person they say I am?" "Is our relationship purely based on physical attraction?" "Does my partner think I'm only in it for financial gain?" " Is she going to leave me if something happens to me?" This leads to a whirlwind of self-doubt and uncertainty about the person you fell in love with.

If you're already in an interracial relationship, you likely understand this struggle, as you've probably faced similar situations. But for those who are confused, here's a short explanation of a real-life scenario that actually happened.

Imagine a couple walking down the street—a white, tall, charming man and a beautiful young woman, hand in hand, heading to a restaurant while chatting and enjoying the moment. A random person might shout, "Why are you with him? Aren't there enough brothers for you? You're a disgrace to the Black community."

A handsome Ethiopian man was dating a beautiful German woman. People often commented on their relationship, and she shared with you how these opinions made her feel reduced to a stereotype—similar to how women are portrayed in adult films—both at work and within his Ethiopian and Eritrean communities.

You have a Nigerian friend who is sweet and kind, yet he often encounters stereotypical attitudes from both friends and even his mother-in-law. Then there's your Japanese friend, who is married to a South African, and together they have two beautiful children. One day, she came to me, heartbroken and nearly in tears, unsure of what to do. "I sent my daughter to the playground with the nanny, and they wouldn't let her in," she explained. To provide some context, they live in a predominantly white neighborhood. Should she have been upset? Absolutely! As a protective mother, she was furious because someone had hurt her child. Lastly, you're married to a German man and are constantly asked, "So, how cold-hearted are Germans?"

You're walking out of a large household store with your German husband when the guard stops you, requesting to check your purse and receipts, while he strolls out without a second glance. Then there's your Italian girlfriend — people constantly ask, "You have quiet a girl, but she must be loud, right?" or "She must be disrespectful to you as an Ethiopian man, right?" Another friend of yours, a young couple with two kids aged 5 and 10, is Swiss, while his wife is from Mozambique. She shared how her mother-in-law treats her as though she's so incompetent that she can't even use a microwave, attempting to "educate" her. Keep in mind, this 70-year-old woman is trying to teach a millennial mother who has already raised two kids how to quickly warm food in the fast-paced lifestyle of Berlin!

They sign up their kids to German school since they couldn't find another European school that would work for their curriculum and get mistreated that they are not German enough to be part of the school.

These situations can really get under your skin, and they happen to many people across various races and cultures. That is the world we live in. However, it's up to you to ruin your relationships or step up and take control of your happy life. For this, you will need to master the art of not caring. If you care too much, you lose, and they win. In the end, everyone wants to win in life. So, how do you master that? How do you develop a thick skin so that opinions, suggestions, and unsolicited family advice don't bother you? Let's dive into it, shall we?

Know What to Do Next

Know Where You Stand

Listen up! Once you've been dating for at least a year and it's not just a casual fling, this relationship is moving towards something real and serious. Save yourself the time and frustration—either end it now or stop resisting and embrace the beautiful yet challenging unity between the two of you. Get in the game and stand by your partner. Stop acting indifferent in front of your friends, laughing at jokes about your partner, or making fun of them, whether it's in front of others or behind their backs. This will only backfire on both of you. Start learning to stand by each other. Eventually, your family and friends may fade away, and he or she will become your true family.

Know Who You Are

Understand who you are and recognize that you have a unique destiny to fulfill. No wave can knock you down if you are firmly anchored to your truth and who you are deep down in your inner self. Your anchor should be just that — not your appearance, race, finances, or the approval of others. The only approval you need is from that energy within. Stop undermining your worth by letting those who had no part in your creation dictate how you see yourself.

Accept Who You Are

You are the only version of yourself this world will ever know. You are genetically unique — there is only one you. Your thoughts, your background, your appearance, and your skills are all distinct. Embrace that. Understand that you are beautifully, uniquely, and wonderfully made. Everything about you has a purpose. My anatomy teacher used to tell the boys in the classroom, "Do you think the girls were created with wide hips and breasts for your visual pleasure? No! It's for nature's design to nurture and give birth, ensuring the continuation of humanity." He would smile and continue explaining the science behind the attraction between men and women. To truly understand this, you must accept that the way you were created serves a greater purpose. Embrace your flaws; they exist to help you find the right match, just like pieces of a puzzle. When you notice a missing piece, you compare it to others to find the perfect fit. Accept yourself as you are!

Your experiences, pains, and life's journey have prepared you for the next steps in your path ahead.

Own Your Choice

You chose to be in a relationship with someone outside your tribe—own it! Don't feel ashamed; be proud! Be proud of your partner. Don't waste your time trying to convince others that your choice is valid or justifying why you're in love. Just own it and enjoy it. Let's be honest: people are going to question you no matter what. Why do you work out so much? Why don't you go out more? Why aren't you studying engineering instead of accounting? Why are you dating this person when you could date so many others? People will always ask questions. If you don't stay grounded and trust that your choices are right for you, you'll end up being tossed around like a football, never reaching your goals in life. Make your choice—and own it.

Don't Be Afraid to Speak Up

If someone makes a comment that bothers you, speak up! If a family member makes an inappropriate remark during a gathering, address it right then and there. Letting these comments slide will only lead to them piling up. Set clear boundaries and address the issue immediately. Don't worry about sparing their feelings; express your thoughts politely but firmly. The longer you let it fester, the harder it will be, and resentment will begin to grow. Speak up and move on.

At a family gathering, a guest who was married to a charming Black American man and had two boys was targeted by a sarcastic comment. One lady, in a mocking tone, said, "Oh, at least the boys didn't get his nose; they look better, more Ethiopian." At that moment, you could see her blood boil and the pain in her eyes. She forced a smile as everyone laughed and slowly walked away, pretending to head to the kitchen. Ten years later, the sting of that moment still lingers.

So, when someone makes a hurtful remark, don't just smile and walk away. Stand up for yourself. Speak up and let them know it's not acceptable. They need to understand. Some people may not be intentionally ignorant but simply unaware. Stay calm, take a deep breath, and make your voice heard.

Know It Takes Time

Building resilience is much like developing and maintaining muscle—it requires consistent effort, sweat, and pushing through challenges. Just like at the gym, you'll need to gradually increase your strength by practicing, adapting, and pushing through moments of discomfort. This process helps you develop what's often called "thick skin" or the ability to stay "unbothered." Without this, the pressures of the world will eventually take their toll. Commit to this journey today, keep going tomorrow, and repeat the cycle. Stay consistent, nourish yourself with the right mindset, and keep executing.

Understanding You Need Grace and Love From Those in Your Life

We all crave love and understanding, especially during tough times. You deserve to experience that grace in your life. The grace you are given freely—allow it for yourself, whether it comes from within your own spirit or from others. Finding people who uplift and energize you—those who leave you feeling lighter and happier after spending time together—is a true blessing. Cherish those relationships. However, if you have colleagues, friends, or even family members who constantly judge, make you feel unloved, or misunderstood, it's important to set boundaries. Give grace as it is given to you, but don't lose yourself in negative energy while trying to offer it to others. Reduce the time you spend with them, as their negativity can slowly drain you and make you question your worth. If you're speaking to them daily, try cutting it down to once a week. When you meet, keep it brief, perhaps just thirty minutes, especially if it's a family member you can't completely cut out. For others, it's okay to walk away entirely. Protect your peace.

Live Your Life, Honey!

This interracial life is beautiful, exciting, passionate, and full of romance all at once. It may be something new for you, your community, or your family, but so what? New is fresh, unique, and full of possibility. Who wants to wear the same outfit every day? Life would be dull if everyone looked and acted the same. Embrace the unique differences between you and your partner, and savor this wonderfully challenging journey, no matter what. Don't let obstacles weigh you down. Don't let the misunderstandings of others make you feel guilty or unworthy of enjoying this beautiful life.

So, what actions and why?

Without a doubt, this book has the power to transform your life. When your journey first began, you may have had a negative outlook. People didn't really understand when you said you had no clue about certain aspects of life, especially when you left home, feeling completely unprepared for the world and unsure of how to navigate it. You could have learned the hard way, enduring tearful, traumatic, and discouraging days, questioning what it was all for. Or, you could learn from others' experiences—avoiding heartbreak and disappointment by reading books like this. This is exactly the path you're taking now.

The reality is, at times, you almost lose yourself in the process of coping—recklessly shopping to fill the void left by heartbreak and drinking more wine than you should to escape the painful conversations and ignorance surrounding you. You spend countless hours trying to prove your worth and capabilities, all while working tirelessly to provide for your family, yet running on empty, both emotionally and physically. At night, the worries consume you: "Have I made a mistake?" "Will my kids be okay?" "Should I already start teaching them about racism?" "How will I protect them if they're bullied?" "I wish my parents were here." "Will I ever see my family again?" "Do my loved ones still care?" Then, you wake up early the next morning, ready to face your responsibilities, even as the weight of it all lingers.

You might be the type of person who doesn't want to burden others with your problems. So you say nothing, not to worry anyone. Assuming you are a strong person, they will ask for help when needed, which you don't do when you need it. Now, you choose to help others at the cost of your own well-being. Eventually, some end up falling into anxiety and depression, and some in self-numbing behaviors. Some do unpleasant things more to cope with things in life. No one wants that to happen for themselves; that's why we are learning. To prevent and deal with what happens.

Now that we've learned some valuable lessons, let's explore the insights you can gain from both the good and bad days. This will help you take control of your own life rather than being overwhelmed by your situations or the problems of your friends, family, or partner. Most importantly, prevents you from those consequences mentioned above.

Open your heart and mind to honestly evaluate whether what you're doing is truly beneficial for you. Be honest with yourself about your current situation. Practice mindfulness to recognize which relationships are contributing to a negative state of mind. Assess whether the relationships you're nurturing are offering you the same sense of support and nourishment in return. This awareness is key to avoiding the bitterness that comes from being used and discarded, like a chewed-up piece of gum. Some people will take everything they can from you, only to move on once they feel they've gotten all they need or believe you have nothing left to offer. You've probably encountered those who claim to be there for you only to betray you behind your back. The reality is that the only person you can truly rely on is yourself. However, even with yourself, there are limits to what you can depend on. Remember this: Everyone lies. Stay aware of others' intentions; only then can you free your mind and live with genuine joy.

Unchain Yourself – Speak Up

Chains can take many forms. There's the chain of expectations from yourself and your family, and the societal expectations that dictate what you should or shouldn't do. There can also be addictions—whether to approval, workaholism, alcohol, smoking, or drugs—as a way to numb your pain. Fear can be another chain, keeping you bound by the worry that things won't turn out well. These various chains can hold you captive, like prisoners.

In life, everyone faces disappointments, loss, betrayal, heartbreaks, rejection, and backstabbing, which is hard to forgive and forget. You feel disappointed that they seemed to take joy in your struggles while pursuing their own dreams. It became increasingly difficult to communicate with them, as they often excluded you from conversations, making you feel unloved, unappreciated, and rejected. You realize you have made numerous sacrifices, yet they viewed it as their right to take whatever they wanted from you. These things happen enormously in mixed couple and mixed family relationships.

This is caused by failing to set boundaries from the beginning, leading to damaging consequences for your life and relationships. You realized you had made a mistake by not speaking up, being a people pleaser, and putting others first. Now, when you try to express how you feel, it is new for them. They dismissed your opinion, claiming it was the "devil" influencing your words.

In this scenario, society and those closest to you have the power to either uplift or crush you. Make sure the decisions you make do not compromise your finances, life, or career plans before making major sacrifices. You can say no and still love them. Avoid running on empty gas so you don't lose yourself. If they genuinely care about you, they will understand and respect your boundaries. If they don't, it's important to speak up and let them go.

After countless arguments, there may come a point when they need nothing from you. They only reach out when they want something, and you start feeling like an outsider. When you're running on empty, tensions build up, often leading to hurtful words and insults. It becomes particularly difficult when you tell them you can't lend more money because you're focused on building a future for your children. This is exactly where the boundary should be drawn from the start. If someone truly loves you, they should care about your well-being, even if they don't share the same interests or values. Otherwise, they're simply exploiting your emotional and financial resources, only to discard you like a used-up cardboard box once they've taken all they can. It's time to break free from these types of commitments that drain your energy and no longer serve you.

So, focus on building your own life first. No matter how much you try to comfort them or arrange things in a way that pleases them, sometimes it is never enough until you say that's enough now! So, prioritize your own needs. This leads us to the next point:

Empower Yourself: Protect Your Inner Strength and Resources

You're Shadow Banned Until You Become Somebody.

No one wants you around when you have nothing to offer — be it time or resources. When you don't stand on your own, you can feel like a nobody to them. So, become somebody first. Focus on building a life for yourself first — pursue that dream job, grow that business — before extending help to others. The reality is that people often only seem to value or seek a relationship with you when you're thriving and doing well. You don't want to wake up later in life and regret investing all your finances and energy into helping your immediate family and friends only to realize you have no one around to support your own dreams. Make sure you establish your own stability before you start sacrificing your time, savings, and energy for others. Recognize who is draining your joy — those who take without offering anything in return. It's okay to love them from a distance, even if they don't understand. Ensure that your time, energy, and finances are invested in things that propel you forward in life. Prioritize your growth because only when you're fully content and fulfilled can you truly give to others. Don't sacrifice your personal development for the sake of others.

Is it Love or Transactional Relation?

Whether we like to admit it or not, all relationships are transactional — whether they're within monocultural or multicultural families or between people from different cultures or countries. It's a common misconception that only mixed couples have transactional dynamics. In reality, history shows that all marriages, regardless of background, have been transactional in some form. Every type of relationship — whether it's work, family, business partnerships, marriage, or even with our pets — functions on some level of exchange. The key difference lies in the "exchange rate" and "exchange type" — how much one person gives to get something in return. What kind of support does one person need to provide to the other? Sometimes, one person contributes little and gets more, and other times, it's the other way around. This dynamic plays out even in everyday conversations. For example, when someone hires you or pays you, they often act as though they hold some level of control. The idea that "love comes first" is a myth. In reality, every relationship is transactional in some form, even if it's not in money — whether through favors, kind gestures, or other exchanges.

Have you ever noticed the old "follow for follow back" trend on social media? People's behavior can be quite amusing. Many times, it's about oneself first. The idea of doing something for someone just to brighten their day or ease their burdens rarely crosses our minds. Instead, we're usually more focused on what we can get from it. If you want to understand human behavior, just watch kids. They're the perfect example of "me, me, me" — claiming what's theirs, comparing who has more, and bargaining with "If you give me this, I'll give you that." They're straightforward with their desires, driven by a sense of ownership and competition. It's fascinating to watch because, in those moments, their actions reflect the true human nature. As adults, we start hiding these behind more sophisticated tactics, but at the core, it's still all about transactions — what we can gain for ourselves, even if it means stepping on others to get it.

When it comes to relationships, the sooner you accept that they're all transactional, the fewer expectations you'll have. And as you all know, expectations often lead to disappointment. By adjusting our mindset, we can spare ourselves from unnecessary heartache. For instance, if you keep doing things your boss disapproves of, you risk getting fired. Similarly, if you ignore your wife's need to feel heard, she might start seeking attention elsewhere, and over time, she may no longer want to stay with you.

Research increasingly suggests that historically, marriage wasn't centered around love. Instead, it was often about practical matters—such as childbearing, political alliances, and uniting kingdoms to avoid wars. The focus was on securing resources, power, and stability, with love being a secondary concern. In this context, marriage could be seen as a transactional arrangement.

Similarly, when a person's values clash with those of others in a family, or when a parent doesn't support your career choices, they may begin to distance themselves and gravitate toward those who share similar beliefs. This isn't just about the emotional discomfort of differing opinions; it's also rooted in human nature, which can shift into a fight-or-flight mode when confronted with opposing perspectives. Once relationships become purely transactional and avoid difficult but necessary conversations, it becomes challenging to restore genuine connection, harmony, and joy. The emotional bond weakens, leaving behind a more practical and less fulfilling dynamic.

Can we break free from this transaction mindset? Yes, but not entirely. But you can have your peace of mind without compromising your needs. Partnerships can find a balance by acknowledging that there is a transactional element in every relationship while recognizing that it can't be the only aspect. Whether it's roles, finances, or emotional exchanges, there's also a deeper layer of passion, connection, love, and shared dreams. This isn't just true for mixed couples—it applies to all relationships that every human being experiences. The key is to recognize that every relationship—whether it's built on love, friendship, or good intentions—has a transactional component. Understanding this allows you to stop expecting things that aren't being exchanged and stop feeling hurt when things don't go how you want. For example, instead of asking, "How could he do this to me? He's supposed to be my friend!" or "Anyone else could do this, but her?" leading you to disappointment. Only to realize that we all have needs and wants in relationships, and so does everyone else. Avoid expecting and assuming. Communicate your needs in a productive manner.

When you understand that relationships are partly about give-and-take, you free yourself from unnecessary heartache. Recognizing that you want something from others—and that they want something from you—helps you manage expectations. And when both parties are satisfied with the exchange, that's when you'll find yourself in a happy, healthy, balanced relationship.

Core Lesson

You find freedom when you stop seeking approval and start living your truth with strength and grace.

3

Building a Strong Foundation: Preparation, Learning, and Growth

Readiness Matters – What's on the ground

Life is an ongoing lesson, constantly teaching you something—unless you're already teaching someone else. Despite language barriers, unclear communication habits, and cultural differences, it can still be difficult to express your ideas clearly. You speak and act with the hope that the listener understands exactly what you meant. Some practice, while others watch YouTube videos, trying to figure out how to communicate better with people from different backgrounds—whether it's Africans, Europeans, Americans, or Asians. At work, you aim to help others understand how things work in Ethiopia, but sometimes they need you to learn their way. Ultimately, the goal is the same: to accomplish the task at hand.

In relationships, it's often the same. At times, you may not be ready to learn, and instead, you may feel the urge to teach your partner how you want things done — how to be more like you, do what you do, or enjoy what you love. This is especially true if you're a parent, particularly with younger kids. You see it clearly every day — the struggle not to argue over small things they forgot to do or the frustration when they're not ready on time. Some days, you're overwhelmed trying to make sure you're prepared or ensuring your kids are ready for tests, school, and life — all at once.

Have you ever had to do something before you were truly ready? It's like being told to take a test or sit for an exam without any preparation. Sometimes, things happen unexpectedly, without any warning. On a typical day, when you know what to expect or have studied well for an exam, you feel confident and ready. But in a surprise situation, you may feel deceived, anxious, and agitated. Life can be like that. It can be something as simple as your child suddenly falling ill and needing to be picked up right when you have an important meeting. That can leave you feeling overwhelmed and stressed. Some days, the pressure builds up, and it becomes easy to snap at your loved ones over small things, only to regret it later when you realize it wasn't worth getting so upset over. These unexpected moments can really get under our skin. That's why you need to train your mind to expect the unexpected.

What if you already knew what to expect? Can you imagine how psychologically and emotionally you would be ready? And you set your mind, "ok, I know they won't take the trash out by the time I am home, and it's ok." "Some days, people would forget to do things." And just set it on so it does not affect your mood. Intentionally saying to yourself, "I am not going to rush today." You say to yourself in the morning, "I know things that potentially could happen, so I am not surprised when it happens." You set intentions to learn things as they come and educate your loved ones instead of snapping at them. You choose to have the upper hand in your day instead of situations controlling how you start the day. Certain things are expected, and they would not get under your skin to the point of potentially leading to emotional reactions or actions, further preventing emotional breakdown.

The same principle applies when preparing for a trip to another country or city or even for work. Before you leave, you often ask yourself, "Did I take care of everything I needed to do? Do I have everything I need?" You think you've got it all covered, but once you arrive, you realize something is missing—and it feels uncomfortable and unsettling. Similarly, not being fully prepared or lacking essentials before making a big life transition can leave you feeling uncertain and anxious. This is why it's crucial to communicate openly and learn from each other during the dating phase. By discussing your needs and expectations early on, you'll be better prepared and able to navigate your journey together more easily, bringing us back to the importance of learning and educating ourselves.

Learn and Educate

We all face the reality of feeling unprepared and anxious about change, yet in today's world, information is abundant, flowing through every channel. However, we often educate ourselves on things that have little practical impact on our lives—topics that don't contribute to our personal happiness or performance. While there's endless information about ways to succeed in our careers or make more money, we seldom focus on knowledge directly affecting our daily well-being.

Whether it's a new relationship, adapting to a different culture, having a baby, entering marriage, or dealing with challenging in-laws, we often feel unprepared for the hurdles ahead. But preparation is key to avoiding disappointment. You can't simply hope or pray your way through challenges, nor can you expect a casual conversation or a passing thought to solve your problems. Just as you wouldn't show up for a test unprepared and expect to pass, you can't tackle life's challenges without anticipating them and putting in the work to understand and address them.

That is the problem with most people in intercultural relationships. You assume it would work by just going with the flow. So you just "wing it" as it comes, leading to disappointments. You didn't learn it before, and you are not willing to learn now. You are choosing to argue to make your point instead of educating. You judge each other instead of choosing to learn about each other's points. Unlike relationships within the same culture, intercultural relationships require extra effort and a learning process. They come with unique challenges and opportunities that demand us to be proactive and informed. At the very least, take time to visualize the basics in your mind and be prepared for what lies ahead.

Just like the exams, be ready for this new chapter in your life. Consider what you will need, how much emotional and physical investment it will require, and what discussions you might encounter. Imagine what your days will look like, what values and beliefs you'll hold, and how you would approach raising children if you choose to have them — and if so, how many. Consider being mindful of how your partner does things and how things work in their culture. Read about the country's history and culture. Watch movies or documentaries so you understand better.

Pay attention to the little details, too. For instance, would serving pork to my in-laws be acceptable, or would it be intolerable for them? How would you handle a situation where teachers at a predominantly white school mistreat my mixed-race child? It may not be possible to have all the answers now, but knowing what to expect can help you avoid emotional triggers.

It's like preparing for a licensing examination: practicing with thousands of questions versus just reading the notes. Unlike monocultural relationships, this requires thinking twice before you speak. When you understand your ally's perspective, you'll be better equipped to handle situations. By doing so, you shield yourself from heartbreak and failed relationships. You've trained and prepared, which ultimately boosts your chances of success.

Take the time to identify the key questions you need to ask yourself to prepare for potential situations. Practice your responses calmly, and avoid making decisions in haste. Don't let misunderstandings turn into personal attacks on each other's cultures.

Give yourself the space to truly learn about the new person you're inviting into your life—not just as an individual, but also understanding the society they come from. This includes learning about their family, culture, food, and how things are communicated within their community.

You might be wondering, "Why should I go through all this for someone I'm just dating?" The answer is that dating is more than just having fun; it's about truly getting to know each other. Sometimes, in the excitement, we overlook important aspects of the person we should be learning about. Enjoy your time together, but also make sure to do your homework. It can save you a lot of heartbreak, disappointment, and unnecessary arguments later on.

Ready for What's Coming

One of the best ways to stay in control before things overwhelm you is by educating yourself and knowing what to expect. Once you're aware of the challenges and questions this new chapter in life might bring, you can prepare yourself accordingly. By the time those moments arrive, you'll know exactly how to respond. In mixed relationships, here are some key aspects to anticipate and learn about in advance.

Paperwork and Its Costs: Handling paperwork, such as non-marital documents, travel papers, and birth certificates, can be an absolute nightmare. The process is often complicated, costing you both time and money. Each document issued by one country may not be accepted unless verified by another country, which incurs additional verification fees. If one country uses a different language, the specific certificate you provide must be translated into their official language for processing.

For a single verification or translation, you can easily spend between 250 and 650 euros. In the Ethio-German case, for example, obtaining birth certificates for your kids requires sending marriage certificates or non-marital certificates and Ethiopian birth certificates to Germany for translation. After that, they had to be sent back to the embassy to confirm that we were the parents before you finally received them.

In summary, everything costs time, money, and a significant amount of effort just to complete one simple document.

Travel Nightmares: If you are in an intercultural relationship, chances are one of you has family somewhere else in the world. You may want to visit them, or they may want to visit you. Perhaps you're a couple who enjoys traveling during summer holidays or even traveling for work. For example, if you have one of the most powerful passports in the world and are married to someone with one of the least powerful, and you haven't changed your passports or IDs from one to the other, this can lead to significant frustration.

Let's say your kids' school is closed, and you want to go to France for summer break. You'll need to apply for a visa for your partner every time you plan to go somewhere. There's a good chance your visa request will be rejected, and with constant visa and immigration laws changing, the process can be unpredictable, time-consuming, and restrictive. Inviting your parents to visit Switzerland is never easy, and forget about having your siblings attend your wedding. My brother could only attend my sister's wedding via Zoom, and he cried his eyes out. The wedding felt sad because of that, compounded by passport issues involving other family members.

You can choose to update your passports to the most accepted passports of one of those countries right away. And when holidays, choose places where you or your partner are welcomed, and plan to submit your visa applications well in advance to minimize disappointment.

The Cost of Effort for Being Understood: No matter how much effort you put in or how clearly you explain, misunderstandings are inevitable. You may find yourself misunderstood by everyone, including the partner you love. This can create confusion, especially for your children.

Not Belonging: One of the main struggles in intercultural relationships is the heightened sense of not belonging. In comparison to non-intercultural relationships, this relationship would constantly make you feel like you don't belong to the family that you thought you would. You unite in this marriage but feel like an outsider at times. Be prepared for this and find ways to cope. Adjust your expectations accordingly and continuously teach yourself how to handle these feelings.

Feeling Like an Outsider: Wherever you go, one of you may always feel like an outsider. You need to decide whether your home is with your partner and your children if you have them. Make a commitment to support each other, ensuring that one of you always makes the other feel comfortable. Prepare for this dynamic, and your relationship will grow stronger.

Controversial Issues: Whether you are Black, Indigenous, Indian, Arab, or Caucasian, you will likely face racism in some form. This can affect your decision-making as a couple. Your white partner may worry about how you would navigate life in their town without facing discrimination. Similarly, you may be concerned about how your children will feel in predominantly white, Arab, Black, or Indian schools. These issues are inevitable, so prepare accordingly. In later chapters, We will discuss how to navigate these challenges together.

Career Journeys: Whichever country you choose to live in, one of your careers will be affected. One partner may need to make sacrifices for the relationship or the family you are building together. The profession that works best for you in one country would work very badly in another. Sometimes, it might even take you years to get back to that profession when you are moving. Keep that in mind before making adjustments to move. Discuss it beforehand instead of just going there and seeing what you will be doing. Plan ahead.

Choices of Housing and Place of Growing Older: The area you choose to live in is one consideration, while the country you decide to settle in is another. You might feel the need to choose a predominantly white or predominantly Black area; it doesn't matter which side you lean toward, but this choice will require a lot of discussion and compromise.

When it comes to selecting a country, you'll need to consider what is best for your children, your career, and your future plans, such as purchasing a retirement home. Factors like affordability, safety, and comfort will complicate this decision, making it a daunting task.

Language and Religion: This is especially important if you are planning to have children. What will be your family's primary language? Teaching your children both languages will influence the choice of school for them. Additionally, consider how you will raise your children in terms of religion, especially if you have different beliefs or varying levels of commitment within the same faith. For instance, one partner may be Buddhist while the other is deeply Christian, or one may be Christian while the other grew up without any religion, focusing instead on ethics. You might also face situations where one partner is Muslim and the other is Christian. What then? It's essential to think about these questions.

Take a moment to educate yourself about your partner's background, including the norms they grew up with and how they treat their parents. Dive into the details as much as possible. Whether you like it or not, these aspects will surface along the way, and you will need to address them. The more you know, the fewer disappointments you'll encounter. So be prepared. Read about your partner's country, and when you meet their family and friends, engage them in conversations to gain a deeper understanding.

Your Strength Develops — Give It Training and Time

The first time you have arguments in the process of learning, don't be hard on yourself. Don't be hard on your partner, either. Also, not on in-laws. Especially not on your kids. Just like fitness training for muscle growth, consistency and not giving up will be needed. You can't be training for a week and say this is not working, and I am giving up. You want the change, the strength you will need to continue training. Perhaps you are making some mistakes in your alignment while lifting the weights. You teach yourself the correct way. You adjust it next time you do the deadlifts. You keep doing it until you see the changes you aim for. You learn about the nutrition you need to feed your body to see the desired changes. You do that. Eventually, you develop that muscle and strength. Same in your intercultural relationships. You have the basics of the information, how to do it, and what to do. You do it. You keep educating yourself, and you continue to adjust. You continue to implement. And before you know it, you are amazed at how wiser and stronger you have become. You are surprised how strong your relationships have become. So give it training and time. Don't give up just after a few gym sessions. Don't give up just after two or three conversations when it comes to your relationship. It's a matter of consistency in training oneself, execution, and giving it time.

Emotions are Gasoline

There will be many emotions involved in your relationship and the relationships around you. This is partly due to our lack of understanding of the perspectives of those from different countries, including their intentions, expressions, and physical interactions. When these differences are misunderstood or miscommunicated, it can ignite existing issues or stereotypes. Acting based on these triggered emotions can damage both your life and your relationship.

You may feel offended when people make sweeping generalizations like, "Ethiopians love their phones" or "Ethiopians can't do graphic design." Or comments like, "Everything is so dirty in Ethiopia, people don't know how to keep their homes neat," or "The staff stink, don't shower, or use deodorant." Such remarks can hurt because you care deeply about how your country and its people are perceived. As a result, you might react defensively instead of trying to understand the intent behind those comments.

The same applies when people say things like, "Germans are racist, right?" or "They're so rude and mean," or "They're so stingy, they wouldn't even pay for the bill on a date night." It's important to remember that not all Germans are racist or rude, just as not all Americans are uninformed about world affairs. Similarly, not all Africans are lazy, and not all Westerners visit Africa only to take photos and collect donations for personal gain. In reality, many are actively working to create positive change in African communities with genuine intentions.

Likewise, not all Ethiopians are glued to their phones or live in untidy environments. In fact, many also live a luxurious lifestyle. There are countless talented graphic designers, programmers, and professionals among us. It's essential to challenge stereotypes and recognize the diversity within every culture. To maintain a peaceful mind and healthy relationships, it's essential to eliminate stereotypical thinking from your mindset. As someone in a cross-cultural relationship, you shouldn't contribute to reinforcing stereotypes. Bringing those biases into your household and family dynamics only creates unnecessary tension. Making assumptions based on stereotypes is a sign of ignorance—something you've worked hard to overcome through education. Instead of relying on stereotypes, use the knowledge you've gained. If you continue to lean on these assumptions, you'll find yourself burning out and damaging your relationship by adding fuel to the fire, often leading to unnecessary arguments. Make a conscious decision to avoid bias and emotional reactions; instead, process situations based on facts. No one wants to be generalized, so don't generalize yourself, and don't generalize your partner's family and friends, either.

Choose Your Battles

Life is filled with challenges as long as you're here. Whether they're big or small, struggles are a part of the journey. You might face financial issues, relationship troubles, career hurdles, or even the quest for inner peace. Some days will feel like victories, giving you hope and motivation. On other days, you may feel frustrated and defeated, leading to emotional and physical exhaustion.

Let's say your partner doesn't like your favorite traditional food. Should you be offended and insist that everyone in your family should like it? No! Continue cooking it and serve it at the table. Let your children try it and see if they eventually enjoy it. If they don't, let it go—don't make it an issue.

What if the other partner is a messy person? If you have kids who don't pick up after themselves, how do you handle it? Can you handle the issues without allowing them to get deep in you and ruin your day?

Another example involves family members who want to borrow money or who accuse one partner of being a gold digger. These are not your battles. If you don't need to agree to a loan, don't. Finances are a major cause of disagreements among couples and can lead to name-calling and even divorce. If someone says something that bothers you, set your boundaries right away, communicate directly, and move on.

To navigate the ups and downs of intercultural relationships without losing yourself, consider these steps. Most importantly, be cautious about taking advice from those who haven't experienced this life; they lack an understanding of the emotional, mental, and physical challenges of living in an intercultural relationship. Instead, learn from those who have been where you're trying to go. Absorb everything they have to share. The problem arises when we seek advice from people who have never faced the same challenges or come from cultures different from our own. Even marriage counselors or therapists may not be helpful unless they have personal experience or have worked with intercultural couples.

Acknowledge Your Feelings: Accept that it's okay to feel overwhelmed. Recognizing your emotions can help you understand what you're truly dealing with.

Identify the Battles: Take a moment to reflect on what challenges are actually yours to fight. Some conflicts may not deserve your energy, while others may be essential to address.

Set Priorities: Focus on what matters most to you. Decide which battles are worth your time and which can be let go. This can help reduce feelings of being overwhelmed. Set priorities on all resources you have, not just your energy. Hence, it includes financial, material, time, etc.

Create a Support System: Surround yourself with people who uplift you. Lean on friends, family, or professionals who can provide perspective and support in this specific aspect. Find couples or families who are living or have been living in intercultural relationships.

Take Small Steps: Instead of trying to fix everything at once, break down your challenges into smaller, manageable tasks. Tackle one issue at a time to make progress feel achievable.

Practice Self-Care: Ensure you take time for yourself. Whether it's through exercise, meditation, or hobbies, self-care helps replenish your energy. This also gives you time to connect with your true nature, clarity on what you're doing well, and how to navigate life in a way that preserves your joy and happiness.

Reflect and Adjust: Regularly check in with yourself to see how you're handling things. If something isn't working, be open to changing your approach.

Another important thing to remember is that not every battle is worth fighting. Some should be left alone, some require just a little effort, and others demand your full commitment. Be selective about where you invest your energy, and prioritize maintaining healthy relationships with your well-being, partner, children, family, and social circle throughout the journey.

Prioritizing your well-being comes first, followed by handling issues as they arise—simple and straightforward. Here's what you can do: Start by making a list of the issues you encounter, rating each one based on its importance and whether it's worth your time and energy. This is where journaling can be helpful, as it allows you to visualize your journey and reflect on your progress by comparing daily outcomes. Next, eliminate those issues that don't concern you. Don't carry other people's burdens if it disrupts your peace.

Unnecessary battles will drain you emotionally, physically, and financially. Remember, not every issue is your fight. Choose your struggles wisely, and prioritize living a peaceful life.

Core Lesson

Preparation and learning build resilience—growth comes when you train your inner strength with patience.

4

Facing Reality: Challenges, Temptations, and Respect in Relationships

You are not extra special.

If you truly believe that you and your partner are one of a kind, it's time to let go of that idea. As humans, we often tend to think our jobs, our partners, or our children are somehow better than others. There is this thinking of "my relationship is better than yours," "My wife or my husband is better than you," and "my job matters more than what you do." This thought of "one of a kind" is making us all delusional. And when in an intercultural relationship, many tend to think they are exceptional. Not to blame the society, but the way society treats mixed couples can be like royalties. Society sees mixed relationships—whether it's Asian and American, Puerto

Rican and German, or Ethiopian and European — as something special. Not only because of financial assumptions but also because of this bold move he/she made to be part of a completely new society. Powerful thinking and social appreciation put your relationship on peddling stone.

Every culture has its own internal sense of pride, often tied to national identity. For example, Ethiopians may consider themselves the most beautiful people in Africa, while people from Madagascar share similar pride in their heritage. Germans often pride themselves on being the epitome of quality and precision. The same can be said for many Americans, South Africans, and people from other nations. Every culture tends to view its own traits as superior to others, fostering a sense of cultural ego. This mindset strips away humility, encouraging a tendency to belittle others while focusing solely on your own strengths and the perceived flaws of others. Ultimately, it leads to the misguided belief that you are somehow "special."

This mindset isn't just confined to your own thoughts; it can extend to those around you as well. Sometimes, people may inadvertently place one partner above the other, offering more respect to one while diminishing the value of the other. Society is constantly in comparison mode, always measuring one against the other. We teach our children not to compare themselves to others, embrace their unique qualities, and follow their own dreams — not someone else's. Yet, as adults, we often find ourselves trapped in the same cycle of comparison.

It's time to break free from the endless cycle of narcissistic behavior or undervaluing yourself. It's important to appreciate who you are and maintain a healthy sense of ego — not one that's inflated to the point of destruction, but one that reflects a balanced self-image. It's about acknowledging your strengths with gratitude, saying, "I am good at this, and I'm thankful," while also accepting your flaws and embracing them. Recognizing the privileges of where you're from is important, but remembering that you are still a human being is key. Finding that balance — neither too much nor too little — is essential. Once you let go of these limiting beliefs, your relationships will become more fulfilling, and you'll live a more authentic, joyful life.

In relationships, it's easy to fall into the mindset that both you and your partner are uniquely special. However, it's important to set that aside at times and focus on addressing deeper issues or having meaningful conversations, whether with your partner, in-laws, colleagues, or anyone you encounter daily. When you start viewing yourself or your family as more special than your partner, it can negatively impact the relationship. This mindset can inflate one partner's ego while diminishing the other's, ultimately damaging the relationship both as a couple and in other areas of your life. It's crucial to address this dynamic early on in your relationship to ensure a healthy, balanced foundation moving forward.

You might catch yourself thinking, "He's a white man, privileged, while I, coming from one of the poorest countries in Africa, might not deserve certain things because of where I come from." Whether you're from Africa, Asia, or any marginalized region, there are times when you might feel undermined or overlooked. If you let those thoughts sink in and internalize the negativity, it can fuel self-doubt and lead to disappointment and a lack of belief in yourself.

Regardless of whether you're a Caucasian man or woman or of any background, it's essential to pause and reflect on how your actions affect others. The tendency for Africans and Asians to generalize, hate, or discriminate based on stereotypes needs to be broken. It's important to ask yourself, "Is my inflated ego causing harm to others? There's also discrimination within communities, where someone who has lived abroad or is in a cross-cultural relationship may be viewed as "educated" or "respected," even when the person who brings in the income or holds the highest level of education hasn't left their home country. This creates tension, both in the relationship and with those around you.

As a result, your perception of each other can be clouded, and the relationship can begin to feel more like a contractual arrangement than one based on love, adventure, and intimacy. It's as if you're living together like roommates, merely co-parenting instead of sharing a meaningful, fulfilling connection.

At times, stereotypes and assumptions can cause you to view your partner or relationship as flawed. You may start to see the person you once loved as someone who is only in it for financial gain or personal benefit. Don't let others—or even your partner—suggest that your relationship is driven by opportunities, money, status, or the need for acceptance. When situations arise that challenge this belief, address them calmly and openly, ensuring clear communication without causing offense.

You need to mentally prepare yourself for the challenges you and your partner may face. It's easy to start questioning the relationship because of these issues, and before you know it, you may even begin to feel resentment toward your partner or certain people in your life. Address these feelings early, before they take root. Don't let assumptions, stereotypes, or negative thoughts dictate your emotions. Take control of your thoughts, actions, and happiness — they should not depend on others. Start practicing this from the very beginning of your relationship to ensure a healthier and more balanced connection.

Be careful not to treat your partner as a God/Godsend or as a charity case either, and ensure your family and friends don't do the same. Treat everyone with respect, rights, and dignity; all humans are beautifully and wonderfully made. If anyone—whether a partner or someone in your life—fails to uphold this respect, they can exit your life at any time. Protect your well-being, peace, and health; it's simply not worth it.

Respect Your Partner

One of the most important relationships to strengthen is the one with your partner. First, it's essential to build a strong relationship with yourself, followed by your connection with your partner and then with others around you—based on the degree of relevance they hold in your life.

It may seem simple and obvious, but respect is often discussed in broad terms—respect for oneself, respect for life, respect for parents—yet rarely is it emphasized in the context of respecting your partner. Respect is a two-way street: men must honor the women in their lives, and women must genuinely respect their husbands. True respect means demonstrating it both in their presence and when they are absent.

Treat him with kindness both at home and in front of your family and friends. Avoid speaking negatively about him to others. The way you talk about him and present him can shape how they treat him and how they view your relationship over time. If they don't see you as a united front, it becomes easier for negativity to creep in. A less united home is easy to break down. You risk allowing that negativity to take root and start cracking your unity from the bottom up. The same applies in reverse.

As a wife or girlfriend, you may find yourself expressing frustrations about him during arguments, which allows others to form opinions about your relationship. If you need to vent or talk to someone, you can discuss your relationship without exposing him or compromising its integrity.

Similarly, as a husband or boyfriend, when you're having drinks with friends and discussing her life plans or personality, the tone of respect you use matters greatly. Avoid saying anything about her that you wouldn't say in front of her. The way you talk about and treat your partner will influence how others perceive and respect her. This includes refraining from making jokes about her, even if they seem harmless or playful. Never allow negative discussions to undermine your relationship.

It's crucial to recognize from the start that you are a team. While you will eventually become one, whether you act as a team or not, it's better to start operating as a unit early on to avoid unnecessary arguments later. Live, act, and perform as a cohesive unit. If those around you sense a divide in your unity, they may disrespect it, manipulate you, or try to create conflict. Therefore, it's vital to respect your partner and consistently make the choice to uphold that respect in all circumstances. It might be challenging, but like every other aspect of life, it requires practice and persistence. Be intentionally respectful every day.

Handling Disagreements with Your Partner

Disagreements are a natural part of life. We wouldn't know good if there were no bad, nor would we recognize light without darkness. We all have harmonious days, but we also experience moments of conflict. Sometimes, these disagreements help us learn more about each other and build a stronger foundation.

The key is to understand what triggers the arguments, identify the underlying causes of the disagreement, and determine how we handle them. How do we communicate with one another in a way that leads to resolution? How can we express our concerns without damaging the other person's dignity?

Research shows that communication involves more than just the words we use; it also encompasses tone and gestures. It's not just what we say but how we say it. For instance, someone might scream at their partner to express their anger, but that doesn't mean the communication is being received well. In fact, it could cause your partner to feel offended and defensive, as it's a natural human response that triggers the fight-or-flight instinct. So, how do we handle situations where we disagree? Is there a right way to argue?

Here's the first thing to understand: disagreements will definitely happen. In the early stages of a relationship, you may not see it coming. Even at that stage, try to imagine the worst-case scenario in your relationship. Consider what your partner might do that you would dislike or even despise, whether it's a behavior or a belief. Athletes are not only trained to win but also to handle defeat. Military boot camps prepare you to win battles, but they also teach you about death and the loss of comrades. The same applies here. When you prepare for the worst, you equip yourself to handle it. Trainees learn to understand their opponents in detail, strategizing and planning to secure victory. You do the same.

Similarly, relationships require you to understand your partner. When you genuinely understand him or her, you'll know how to communicate effectively in a way that your partner can hear and comprehend. This is what we call productive conversation, which transforms your dynamic from opponent to teammate. In this way, you also prevent unnecessary potential future arguments.

The next crucial step is learning to accept each other. Understand that you are two distinct individuals, each shaped by your own principles and norms, and you must be willing to embrace one another despite those differences. However, this doesn't mean accepting harmful behaviors, such as living with a drug addict or tolerating abusive actions, especially if these have been long-term issues. Ultimately, you're together because you love each other, and if there's a possibility of change, you should care enough to help. Beyond that, allow each other to be your true selves, and together, strive for a better version of yourselves—growing and uplifting one another.

Another practical example:

For my partner, the routine is usually different. Every morning, he has a very thorough cleaning habit that can sometimes be a bit much for our children and me. He exclaims to our kids, "Sauber machen!" ("Clean up!") and "Was ist das hier?!" ("What is this here?!"). At first, it absolutely irritated me. Not only did it disrupt my day, but it also left me feeling a little resentful when he woke up just to say good morning. Some mornings, I'd head out before he woke up, just to find a little calm and avoid the early-morning back-and-forth. I would only return once I knew he had already left for work. Eventually, I decided not to let this interfere with my peace of mind, time efficiency, productivity, or our team spirit. Still, I kept asking myself: "Why is this such a priority for him, to the point that it affects our relationship?" and "Why does he feel the need to clean the moment he wakes up, even before having coffee?"

I've learned that precision and tidy spaces are essential for him, shaped by growing up in Germany. Watching his mum clean around the breakfast table while we were eating made me realize he grew up with a very structured, almost military-like approach to tidiness. These habits are deeply ingrained and influence how he starts his day and approaches life.

On the other hand, the first thing that comes to my mind in the morning isn't cleaning the house. Growing up in Ethiopia, I had helpers at home, and studies always came first. Constant attention to order was new to me. I say to myself, "God, no! Mornings are my favorite and most productive hours." I'm more focused on doing something that moves both him and our family forward, rather than tackling chores. Cleaning is low on my to-do list, something I plan to do after finishing my work for the day. I prefer to take care of household tasks and meal prep for the kids before picking them up. This approach helps me feel at peace with myself and my accomplishments for the day—not just for him. For my partner, the routine looks different: first, clean, then coffee, and then head out. I value seeing how he approaches his day differently, even if it's not my way.

If you are such different types of people and don't accept these differences in how your partner starts their days, you will eventually drift apart. As a couple coming completely from different values communication and clarification is important. You'll need to learn how to express yourself without offending, criticizing, or resorting to name-calling. The solution lies in either accepting each other's differences or recognizing that it won't work. Meet halfway. Make the effort to understand and see things from their perspective. Stay open to change and work on improving what you can.

It could be his love for football or golf or perhaps her desire to have a girls' night out once a month. Maybe he doesn't like going to the gym or looking like the bodybuilders you see there. Perhaps she doesn't enjoy cooking at all. You'll need to find a way to accept these differences and determine what works for you, allowing certain things to go. When you are happy as an individual, you can thrive together.

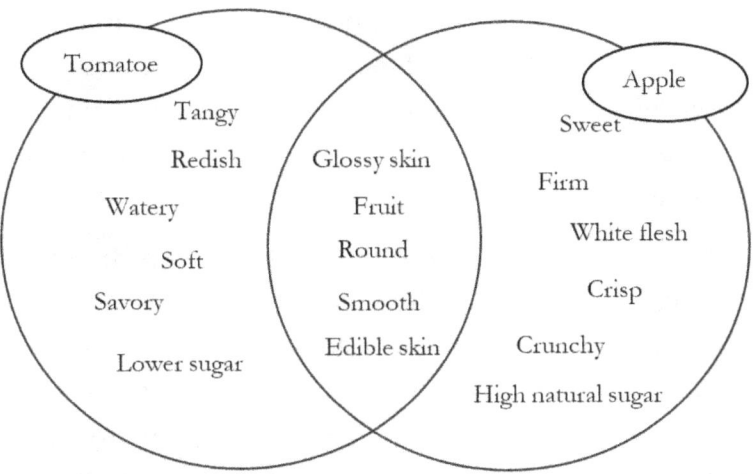

It's like those two circles you learned about in math class — the union and the intersection. There's a part of you that makes you who you are, and you enjoy doing that. Then, there's the part where you come together to find an intersection filled with love, understanding, and acceptance.

Both apples and tomatoes are nutritious food sources, each with its own unique characteristics and benefits. While they share some similarities, they also have distinct traits that make them valuable in their own right. Their differences offer their own advantages, making them beneficial as a whole. What they have in common demonstrates that you don't need to eat the same foods repeatedly to achieve balanced nutrition. If they were completely identical, one wouldn't need the other; instead, you could simply choose another variety of fruit to meet your nutritional needs.

Now, take a look at your life and draw two circles, like the diagram. In each circle, write down the qualities that define you as an individual. Then, list the things you enjoy together or have in common. Consider whether you can accept each other's unique traits—personality, food preferences, favorite sports, and all the little details that make you who you are. Take some time to reflect on it and discuss it over a nice dinner. Sometimes, what your partner offers is exactly what you need in your life, something you don't have. It fits like a missing piece of the puzzle. The differences you each bring can become a strength for the other. Together, make a decision: either embrace these differences or let them go. Clarify what you can't tolerate or live without, and if necessary, end the relationship now to avoid wasting any more years in unhappiness.

Why Are You In It? (Things Fall Apart)

There's a saying in Ethiopian culture: *"hilm teferto sayitay ayitaderem."* It means you shouldn't let the fear of having a bad dream keep you from sleeping. As humans, we constantly fear. We fear financial instability, the future of our children, and engaging in certain activities. What truly matters is how we respond to our fears. We must learn not to take action from a place of fear but rather from a place of faith. Faith in you that you can do it. Trust in your relationship and your partner.

That's why, when we start a business or a new relationship, we often say, "This is the one. This is the business I want to build. The dream I had that will make a difference. This is it!" However, fear kicks in when you see something that seems too good to be true. Or encounter a challenge or slight misunderstanding with your business partner. In those moments, you choose to move forward and keep progressing, or you give up. However, you know that decisions like this major are not to be made when emotions frail up. So, you avoid emotional decisions that lead to giving up.

You take some time to reflect on it. You talk to your therapist or loved ones to gain perspective. Eventually, you regain your clarity and take the necessary steps to heal from challenges and navigate difficult situations. You don't allow obstacles to determine the success of your endeavors. Similarly, you're in the relationship because you believe in it. You don't let fear dictate your connection with your partner. You don't let challenges break you down or tear you apart. Have faith and act in the best interest of your partnership. Don't worry too much about what the future holds in 5 or 10 years. Instead, focus on loving your partner today. Remind yourself why you're with them and the feelings you had when you first met. Reflect on what you've been through together and the beautiful moments you've shared, including your children, if you have any. That's why you're in it. Don't forget that. When doubts arise and you feel like giving up, remind yourself of why you're in it and what it means.

Sometimes, you may feel overwhelmed, as if everything is falling apart. You might question whether entering such a relationship was a mistake, which can bring feelings of failure toward your kids, family, and friends. When challenges come up, it's important to take a step back. Relationships like these can be emotionally draining and demanding. But don't you dare give up! Get back up and take another step forward with faith winning over fear.

You hold on and fight for your relationships, your marriage, and your children. Strong relationships are tested and strengthened in difficult times. When you strive for unwavering resilience, fear should never control your decisions in life or relationships. Challenges and uncertainties are unavoidable, but how you respond to them makes all the difference. Instead of letting fear guide your choices, act with faith in yourself, your partner, and your journey. Take time to reflect, gain perspective, and remind yourself of the reasons you began this path. Whether in business or love, don't let obstacles or doubts lead you to give up. Embrace the challenges, heal from setbacks, and keep moving forward with faith, not fear.

You Will Be Tempted to Give Up

Let's say you are Indian and have met a potential partner from your community. If you like this person, you may envision a future together—marriage, growing old together, and perhaps building a family. This is not arranged but on mutual attraction. People tolerate and accept that. When your partner is from your own tribe, you're less likely to question the relationship compared to one outside your community. That's simply a fact. You might anticipate certain disagreements along the way, but you have to decide to make it work no matter what.

When you're in a relationship with someone from a different background or tribe, disagreements are bound to happen. However, many of us enter these relationships with less clarity than we should. Some may not be open-minded, while others might fear that their partner has hidden motives. At times, you may idealize your partner, only to realize after marriage that they are not as perfect as you once believed. You may even encounter situations where relationships formed in one country, like Ethiopia, become complicated when a partner has a previous marriage and children abroad that was never disclosed.

You might find yourself thinking, "What is going on? I'm not willing to compromise my culture if these same issues persist.

Many people believe that Africans are exceptional in bed, but once the honeymoon phase ends, you might find that it's not as great as you expected. This realization can lead you to doubt whether you really want to continue the relationship, especially if you initially thought your partner was amazing in bed or a great teaser. Most of us also think that the foreign white man *Muzungu (frenji)* would be caring and spoiling you like a queen. Somewhere along the way, you realize that he is another guy who went beyond above to get you, and now he is too lazy to treat you like a queen. Now what? Do you give up?

No, because in the first place, you made the mistake of handing your happiness over to your partner, assuming they were responsible for it. There are two things you need to correct: First, stop letting others' opinions and judgments sway you. Second, remember that your partner is not responsible for your happiness—you are.

No, you don't give up unless you've truly exhausted all possibilities to make it work, or if you're facing abuse—then it's time to look for help and reconsider the whole relationship to begin with. Otherwise, when these realizations hit, remember that your partner isn't being "bad"—they're simply being human, just like you. Initially, when people encounter something new, they treat it with excitement and value. But over time, after they've gotten used to it, the novelty fades, and it doesn't feel as special as it once did. You still appreciate it, but the excitement isn't the same. This is human nature for both you and your partner. So, cut yourselves some slack and enjoy each other.

You Need to be ok with Having No Support System

Just a heads-up: this isn't meant to scare you but to lay out the facts so you can make informed adjustments and decisions for your life. Here is another fact. This life is a life that runs with having mostly no support system but yourself. Friendships are hard to build. Some will take long. Sometimes, it might not happen at all, especially when you are in a certain country. Sometimes, they will assume you are leaving anyway, so why put effort into building friendship to begin with? Scared for their kids to be friends with your kids, thinking they will be heartbroken when you leave the country. The things you will do may not make sense for many when traveling so much. Location changes will make it hard to maintain relationships since you move and travel a lot. If you are working, your only social talk with adults will be with your colleagues. If you have kids, the adult communication you have would be only with other parents. If you are a church person, perhaps you can join a fellowship group. Difficulty finding someone to babysit or help you out with groceries is unimaginable. And unless you have been well established, it will not come easy to have a nanny at hand to make regular arrangements.

Family members live far away to come help you out or help each other out. Somedays, it will be hard to find someone to talk to. Hard to be valuable to your family over the phone, thinking they would be worried. It's not easy to open up to the mum or dad you met at school drop-offs. Some days, it will feel like you have nobody in a country you don't know. You need to be a person who will be okay with being alone and having no one, sometimes having even no one when you are sick, injured, or unable to perform. The special occasions like Christmas, your celebration days, holidays, and the winning days you want to share will feel empty. Your kids' birthdays will feel so alone since you will be the only one singing Happy Birthday. The point is that if you can't handle these things, this life is not for you. Knowing these facts and still wanting to do it, then expect a bit of sadness and depressing moments in your life ahead. Again, not to sadden you, but knowing the hard facts ahead is good for your preparation and for making situations work for you when they happen.

Expect to Get Frustrated

No matter how adaptable you believe you are, both sides of your family — and even your partner — will eventually get on your nerves. This is because you perceive and respond to situations differently. In cross-cultural relationships, certain things can get lost in translation. Even if you're speaking English, which may be a second language for both of you, your different backgrounds still influence the way you communicate despite using the same language. This type of relationship requires constant, mindful communication rather than relying on easy, automatic exchanges.

Then you might get married and have a baby. Then, more conflicts happen sometimes, which happens to be funny. That is why you see so many comedians making jokes about it, including Trevor Noah (south African +Swiss), Zaineb Johnson (Yemeni + American), Rossel Peters (Indian + Canadian), Tedros Teclebrhan (Eritrean + German), and many more. One of the funny things you encounter is that the way the newborn and the new mum would be taken care of is different in two distinct cultures. The role of the new father is defined differently. What would both the mothers-in-law do when they visit to help? Their ideas about what would help would vary. Sometimes, their approaches would be completely opposite.

In German culture, it's common to open windows to let in fresh air, while in Ethiopian culture, it's preferred to keep everything closed and dark during the postpartum period. Lying in bed with your newborn crying nonstop, and those two ladies would be driving you crazy in your postpartum days. One would make tea to help boost my milk supply, while the other would prepare *Atmit*, a traditional Ethiopian drink. By the time your husband comes home, evenings would inevitably turn into uncomfortable conversations as you try to explain why one was completely wrong and the other was right. There are countless incidents like this, but it's important to remember that there are always two sides to every situation—and there always will be. Above all, understand that these misunderstandings and miscommunications will test your patience, but both of them truly mean well.

Different cultures define success in their own unique ways. Your German father might view the job you're doing as silly or pointless, while your mother from Ethiopia sees it as an accomplishment. They may make comments that devalue what you believe you've achieved, but those are based on their own perceptions. While the other says "well done," It can be confusing. It can be upsetting or frustrating, but it doesn't mean you have to let it turn into resentment or cause you to hate what you love doing. One of the key lessons these experiences teach is the importance of embracing differences, acknowledging different opinions, and choosing to live together in harmony.

Family members can sometimes be more clueless than you might expect, and you may even find yourself in similar situations along the way. They're constantly learning, just like you are. The same applies to your partner—they may occasionally get on your nerves too. In these relationships, it's important to make a conscious effort to learn about each other continuously. Instead of asking, "How could she act like that?" or "How could he say that?" try to understand where they're coming from.

Keep in mind that all relationships, especially the ones that matter most to you, will come with their challenges. One key reason is that what excites you may not excite them, and they won't share the same enthusiasm for things that don't interest them. The same applies to your definition of success—while you may celebrate certain achievements, you might expect others to share in that celebration. But if they don't view those achievements as success, they won't celebrate them with you. The same goes the other way around. You love them, and they love you, but there will be things they simply won't be excited about if they don't personally find them exciting. Let go of the expectation that they'll always share your excitement, and you'll avoid unnecessary frustration.

Family

You may have lived it or heard how demanding African families can be when one of their members is successful or considered successful. Generally, there are three scenarios.

The first scenario involves a person who finds an excellent job or starts a successful business, allowing them to earn a good income. In this case, the individual is expected to support the family financially during emergencies, pay bills collectively, and send money to relatives on special occasions.

The second scenario occurs when a family member lives abroad. This person is often expected to send money regularly — ideally monthly or quarterly — to support their family. You need to remember your loved ones and show them you care by sending assistance whenever you can. This may include covering medical emergencies, funding home modifications, or supporting siblings and cousins with sudden career needs.

The third scenario involves a family member marrying a foreigner or someone rich, which often leads to the assumption that they are financially prosperous. This can result in requests for career advice, help finding jobs, covering travel expenses, paying medical bills, and writing recommendation letters or invitation letters for family members.

Essentially, you may find yourself with a lot of responsibilities. It will require constant sacrifices and compromises for the needs of others that may not align with your life plan or contribute to your personal growth.

In all these scenarios, you find yourself constantly battling between taking care of yourself and supporting the larger family you love. Pleasing your parents and alleviating their burdens off your community to ensure your siblings achieve success can drain you emotionally, financially, and physically.

You may wake up one day believing you are making progress — studying and working your entire life to improve your situation and leave something for your children — only to realize how little you have advanced because you've been trying to carry the entire family with you. It can feel overwhelming if you attempt to do it alone.

You cannot change the lifestyle of your community and family single-handedly. It's crucial to recognize this early on. One day, you might find that, after helping everyone else, you're burned out and looking for support, only to discover that it's hard to come by. You realize that people can be disappointing; once they have received what they need from you, you may find yourself no longer important to them, and they are nowhere to be found.

Before embarking on the often nerve-wracking and heart-wrenching journey of this new life, which typically begins after your second year of working, it's essential to set boundaries for yourself and those around you. If you need to provide financial support, establish a specific amount each month and encourage them to save it for emergencies in the long run. Make sure not to be completely invested in solving everyone's problem. In many African countries, we have huge family members, sometimes extending to the old friends of our parents and their kids, and so on. Unfortunately, this also goes out to all around the globe when you think about it. Unless your family has been fortunate enough, you would still need to support them in kind or monetary ways. Asian countries like Vietnam, India, Pakistan, and Arab countries, as well as some European countries. This is something that is absolutely inevitable as long as you are on this planet. For this reason, clear communication is essential in your family relationships, and this begins right from the start.

Never turn to family members to solve problems they have no experience with. It's crucial to keep certain matters private between you and your partner—don't involve family, and don't let others do the same. Similarly, family members should not ask your partner for favors without consulting you first.

When it comes to borrowing money, this is a particularly sensitive issue. One idea could be that borrowing is limited to formal institutions like banks, not families, as it has been seen over and over again ruining relations. While this cannot always be applicable, one solution is to set up a separate family account and contribute to it monthly. This way, you'll have funds available for family emergencies without complications arising from borrowing from loved ones.

If someone has extra money to lend, ensure there's a clear agreement on repayment terms, such as a specific monthly amount. However, if borrowing money or making commitments requires sacrificing your plans and needs, it is better to avoid it, as it can build resentment over time, especially when others do not keep their promised payment time and do not understand the impact of your sacrifices.

If you ask most people from African countries, they would give you plenty of examples. But to share something that happened a couple of times, you have been dreaming of changing my car for years. A family member approached you asking to borrow 5 million Ethiopian birr to buy a piece of land he really wants. In this scenario, if you are in a mixed relationship, it would be considered rude to say no. Why wouldn't she help out her family members and relatives with this white man she married? Disregarding that the person is your partner and the implications it has on your relationship. And like every other same-race husband and unit as a marriage, you are trying to build a home. You are trying to make sure you get your retirement plans right. School fees and college finances covered. At times, people don't see it that way, and they still demand it.

This family member would then suggest that he could give up his old Toyota car for the time being. He proposes that he would repay the remainder over time or that we could keep the car as collateral while slowly repaying the debt. In that moment, without letting emotions cloud your judgment, you couldn't help but think about how selfish people can be. If you allow them, you could easily become a stepping stone for their ambitions at the cost of your desire and plans in life.

Reflecting on this situation, wonder whether this proposal truly serves anyone's best interests besides his own. Did this person take the couple's financial well-being into consideration? Can this person really be trusted to value and respect you and your marriage? It's crucial to make the right decisions before family members on either side start getting on your nerves. You don't owe anyone anything. One of the mistakes you can make is not being honest and saying no in clear terms from the beginning. Say yes and do it if you are really sure about it all. When you are hesitant or say let me think about it knowing that you can't do it will be harder than you think. So do it right away.

Bending your life plans for someone who is only focused on their own success — especially at the expense of your family's future — is not the way to go. That kind of person should be kept at a distance.

Friends

Friendship is often considered one of the most important relationships in life. However, if not handled wisely, it can become one that hinders your personal growth and holds you back. It's crucial to pay attention to how the friendship begins and what sustains it, as these factors can play a significant role in its impact on your life. Most relationships begin with a certain amount of doubt. You meet someone, your energies align, and you think, "Maybe this could grow into something amazing, or it might be a complete disaster." At the early stages of a relationship, no one can truly predict how things will unfold. We all want to be understood, and you might say, "Oh my God, this person gets it. He understands my challenges and adventures."

Initially, there's often a playful phase where friends mock this new person, and you share laughs over funny things that connect you. As months pass and you enter a relationship, friends may want to know more about this new person and express their concerns or seek approval. Soon, you all hang out together—his and her friends combined.

That's when problems arise, especially due to significant cultural differences or someone doing something incredibly inappropriate.

This is the situation. Once you start inviting people over and going out together, ridiculous things start happening. On a random Saturday night, you would have your usual gathering at your place and eventually decide to go dancing. You all drive together to a bar known for its great music and agree to sit by the bar until the dance floor is heated up.

When you arrive, the place is packed, and your only option is to stay near the bartender. You order a bottle of whiskey, and everyone is having a good time—some friends from school even drop by, adding to the fun. As the night went on, people began dancing, but they started leaving one by one without settling their bills. You find yourself standing there, looking around for any of your "friends," but everyone left.

Suddenly, you're stuck with the bill with thousands to pay. Long story short, your sister's boyfriend and your new boyfriend end up having to cover the entire tab.

Would you call them friends? Do they deserve to be part of your life?

There's this friend of yours. You work together. This person only calls you or wants to meet up when he needs you onboard on new proposals because you look good on paper and you are Caucasian. Would you call that a friendship or partnership in business? You need to know what friendship means.

Not to forget that there are scenarios where a friendship turns into dating. Or you meet someone, and you start dating. Sometimes, people do the dating to end up in marriage for visa purposes. Not all, but at times, once they get the visa or the residency he/she will dump you and go back to dating someone from her/his own country.

You may have heard or seen many stories like these and might even have plenty more to share. The most important thing to keep in mind is that some friends will use you and lie to you. Especially in a mixed relationship and the other person is from a Western country, all finances will be on you. You are expected to invite everyone regardless of whether you know them or not. Such relationships can drain you emotionally and financially, leading to bitterness until you learn to forgive and restore peace to your heart. So, heads up. Be mindful of who you let in your circle.

Pay attention and let go of anyone who raises red flags at the first sign of trouble. While some people say to give second chances, I believe not everyone deserves one — only those who truly matter in your life. Only to those who you are sure have good love and intentions for you. Be mindful and let off those if what they are doing slightly doesn't feel right. Remember, people come, and people go. It goes the same for any friendship you encounter along the way. Just because a friend was there during one season of your life doesn't mean they need to be in the next chapter.

Some people can be clingy, and it's important to shake them off and keep only those who truly matter and have your best interests at heart. Those who are constantly looking to take advantage of you will drain your energy like ticks. Let go of them and run. Do not give them any access to your life in any way.

Balancing Family, Culture, and Travel Frustrations

Missing Social Occasions & Inability to Travel Visit Family

You may genuinely want to visit a family member in a Western country and return home afterward. You have no intention of settling in Europe, the UK, the US, or Canada, but there's a chance you may not be able to see your sister, your parent, or your partner, even though you're financially stable and hold a good social status. This is because the actions of a few people from your country have caused negative perceptions that affect the image of your homeland, and unfortunately, your family — including your children — will face the consequences. The wrongdoings of one often reflect on others. Many people go through numerous attempts, sometimes ten or more, to get a visa to reunite with family in the United States. Meanwhile, some individuals from developing countries abuse the system by claiming false asylum without proper documentation, causing developed countries to tighten their security measures to protect their resources and societies. This situation makes it difficult for couples with children to visit family, participate in holidays, and attend important social occasions, causing heartbreak for many. As a result, some families are forced to change passports in order to travel freely as a unit. This creates unnecessary barriers and disruptions, preventing families from being together during important moments. It's not because those who need support from Western countries don't deserve it, but rather because some individuals misuse these opportunities, leaving many others unsupported, divided, and facing unnecessary travel logistics and rejections. Many don't realize the impact of their actions on the image of their home countries or the broader consequences between the two countries. What once worked well is now affected by the actions of individuals, showing how each person's choices can influence a larger scale.

How National Perceptions Influence Your Actions

Some countries make you feel instantly accepted, while others—surprisingly—can make you feel like a second-class citizen, even in your own home country. One person once shared that they feel more at ease arriving in the United States than returning home. The warmth, respect, and friendly smiles in the U.S. made them feel valued, and they'd rather stay there than return to a place where they would be treated poorly. Unfortunately, this is a common experience in many developing countries. Even if someone is a leader, changing lives and being the humblest person you could meet, they might still be treated as less important because of their appearance or accent. Meanwhile, those who seem wealthy or come from developed countries are often given more respect, regardless of their actual worth or character.

This bias can be even more pronounced depending on your gender. In many cases, being a man or a woman changes the way you're treated. This same mentality affects global issues such as visas and freedom of movement.

As an African woman traveling alone, you might find yourself randomly stopped for a check, even after passing through security. Your bag might be searched without warning, and you may face inappropriate comments or unwanted attention. This behavior often comes from assumptions about "sex tourism" — an uncomfortable stereotype. Similarly, as a Black man, you may feel uneasy around customs officers, even when you're doing nothing wrong. It happens to many of us, and it's an uncomfortable reality.

Even when flying business class or heading to the business lounge, you might notice people watching you, sizing you up as if you don't belong. It makes you question whether you're really free or if you're just living in a false sense of freedom. Often, it feels like someone is always waiting for you to make a mistake or misstep.

All of this stems from deep-seated historical biases, shifting rules, and constantly changing regulations. There always seems to be something that could derail your trip, and it's essential to prepare for the unexpected. Having a plan B is crucial because, in many cases, nothing is constant. Many more problems. But how can we address this?

The most effective way to address these issues is through cultural awareness and education, helping individuals understand the long-term consequences of their actions on society, which can deeply impact future generations in a negative way. The well-being of all humans on this planet is interconnected. We've seen this repeatedly through pandemics, wars, and how the decisions of one country can affect the entire world. This interconnectedness exists on a larger scale and within smaller settings like our homes. Negative experiences and hatred can slowly grow within generations, ultimately leading to catastrophic consequences worldwide.

Equally important in ensuring equal freedom of movement is adopting a fairer approach that focuses on encouraging positive actions rather than only highlighting the negative ones. Education and cultural awareness should also extend to individuals involved in travel experiences. As a traveler, it's essential to mentally prepare for biases and be resilient, striving to be the most unoffendable person you can be.

Cultural Norms and Values

As humans, we have an inherent need for a sense of belonging to certain tribes and communities. Since the dawn of humanity, we have claimed land or colonized others' territories, calling them our own. Culture is a crucial aspect of our identity, shaped by both formal laws and unwritten values that we expect others to honor if they wish to be part of our community. When someone speaks disrespectfully or behaves inappropriately, we feel offended or disrespected.

These cultural norms can dictate various aspects of life, such as how we behave in public, dress, eat, or even pay at the supermarket. When you study these norms, it's fascinating to discover what is deemed acceptable, encouraged, and tolerable across different cultures. Certain things that are normal are totally unacceptable. What may be seen as rude in one culture could be the only way to get things done in another. For example, some cultures are comfortable speaking to each other in a loud, direct, or seemingly aggressive manner, while in others, this could be perceived as deeply disrespectful and potentially lead to a serious confrontation.

Living in a country different from your own or marrying someone from a different cultural background is a constant learning experience filled with inevitable mistakes. Just when you think you've figured out one aspect of their culture, another lesson presents itself. This ongoing process can make relationships with your partner and those around you both fun and exciting. However, there are moments when you might think, "I don't even know this person," or "I never knew this side of them—if I had, I might not have married them." If you're lucky, or if you make an effort to truly understand each other from the start, you can navigate these cultural differences without frustration or the fear of disappointing your partner or others.

To help you understand better, consider the practical examples provided in this book. Living in different countries, whether for short or long-term stays, teaches you a lot over the years. Gaining knowledge through experience is valuable, but understanding the importance of doing some research before arriving in a new country is even better and crucial— there are things we should all learn earlier before it negatively impacts us. So, before we dive into the next topic, here are a few fun and essential facts to keep in mind when meeting, dating, living with, or marrying someone from any of the countries listed below.

Simple Fun Facts to Remember: in comparison to the others, not all but just a few of the countries from experience:

Ethiopia: In Ethiopia, greetings are an essential part of starting any conversation, and it's customary to greet others before making requests. Modesty in dress is highly valued, and it's important to avoid revealing or inappropriate clothing, particularly in public. Showing respect for elders is crucial, and offering help when needed is greatly appreciated.

When shopping, negotiating for a discount is common, but it's generally less intense than the bargaining you might experience in Indian or Pakistani markets. Communication tends to be indirect, especially when discussing sensitive topics, so it's important to approach conversations with tact and respect.

Religion holds significant importance in Ethiopia, and it's essential to be respectful and mindful of local customs, particularly when attending religious events or being invited to religious gatherings. Always approach these occasions with sensitivity to the local norms.

When using public transportation, it's common to lean on someone's leg for support while getting on a taxi or bus, and this is not viewed as an invasion of personal space. It's simply seen as a gesture of communal support, and it's perfectly acceptable. Ethiopians look out for one another, and you may find that if you need assistance on the street, there's often someone ready to lend a hand.

If you're approached by someone asking for money, especially near religious or prayer areas, it's customary to give. Similarly, parking attendants typically expect a small tip of 10 to 50 birr at each stop. Tipping plays an important role in getting things done, so it's wise to have small changes ready when visiting public places or receiving services.

South Africa: In some communities, particularly among people of the same tribe, it's customary to greet each other, even when passing on the streets. It's common to address one another as "sisi" (sister) or "bru" (brother), signifying a close familial bond. This practice is usually limited to the Black and colored communities and does not typically extend to the white community. Conversations on this subject can become intense, as the trauma from past histories is still in the process of healing for many in society. It's also a sensitive topic among colleagues and friends from mixed communities.

Similarly to Ethiopia, it's not unusual for colleagues, employees, or even friends to ask for a loan, sometimes simply as a gift, other times with a verbal agreement to repay. This is not seen as shameful but rather as a way to support one another when there's extra to share. It's not necessarily because they are in need but rather because the desire for more—especially in terms of wealth and status—is highly valued. Owning cars and large homes holds significant social importance in these cultures.

Germany: Communication is very direct; there's no sugarcoating it to make it more comfortable for you to hear. Facts are presented as they are, which can often come across as rude. In most cases, you must earn money before others will consider giving it to you. The logic is that people need to work for what they receive, and giving small amounts, like 2 euros to a beggar, is not common. Additionally, there is no expectation to pay for someone else's bills, even if they are friends of your partner or colleagues. This contrasts with situations in Ethiopia, where it is more acceptable to pay for someone's bill, but typically only for yourself or, perhaps, the person you're dating — unless you feel particularly generous.

India: It's acceptable for women to wear clothing that exposes their bellies, but shoulders should remain covered. In Ethiopia, however, it's perfectly normal to wear tops that show shoulders, but showing the belly is a no-go! You do not pay with your left hand as it is considered as bad luck. If you are African, people might ask to touch your hair and comment, "You look beautiful now; you look like an Indian."

Respecting your partner, particularly if you're from India, is crucial. In Indian culture, just like in Ethiopian culture, showing respect to elders holds significant importance. As you transition into adulthood, there's often an expectation to marry, secure a respectable job, and have children — these milestones are seen as markers of success and responsibility.

Japan: Respect for personal space is paramount in Japan. You can't push people around on public transport, and even having your bag accidentally touch someone is considered inconsiderate. It's important to be mindful and respectful in public spaces. When making payments, cash is typically placed on a small tray, not handed directly from hand to hand. Also, it's customary to remove your shoes when entering any building, whether public or private.

Tipping is not practiced in Japan and is seen as rude or even insulting. Instead, service excellence is part of the culture. Payments are often made in cash rather than cards, which differs from practices in countries like Germany or the U.S.

Environmental respect is deeply ingrained in Japanese culture. There are strict penalties for littering, especially for throwing trash into the sea or leaving it in public spaces. Eye contact during conversations is generally avoided, as it can be perceived as disrespectful. Instead, it's polite to slightly lower your gaze, especially when speaking to elders. Like in Ethiopia and India, elders are held in high esteem, but in Japan, the level of respect shown to them is even greater than you might expect.

Pakistan: You don't do handshakes with females if you're a man and vice versa. Family and respect for elder family members are important in the culture. Living with in-laws and your kids and grandkids is normal.

In Jamaica, there are specific cultural practices around gender and marriage. For example, married women are traditionally not allowed to sleep next to their husbands while menstruating, as part of the cultural norms around cleanliness and rituals.

When it comes to punctuality, it is not as strictly observed, much like in Ethiopia. Family events or gatherings tend to be very relaxed, and it's not uncommon for them to start later than the planned time, with a laid-back, easy-going approach to scheduling.

American: Unlike Japanese culture, where tipping is not customary, tipping in the U.S. is expected in most service industries, with 15% to 20% being the standard. Service quality is typically excellent, as customer satisfaction is a top priority — truly, the customer is king! In terms of dress code, public attire is generally very casual, with people opting for comfort over formality. This is in stark contrast to Germany, where the way you dress in public holds significant value, and people tend to dress more neatly and formally.

Another key difference is the role of small talk. In the U.S., engaging in light conversation about topics like sports, the weather, or current events is common, even with strangers. However, in Germany, small talk with random people, such as those in supermarkets or at cash registers, is rare, and interactions tend to be more straightforward and reserved.

Personal space is highly respected in both countries, but in the U.S., it's considered rude to stare at others, and people tend to avoid any uncomfortable physical proximity. For example, on public transportation, you typically wouldn't sit next to someone on a bus or train if there are other empty seats available. Lastly, in the U.S., the "bigger is better" mentality prevails, especially when dining. Be cautious when ordering meals at restaurants or cafes, as portions tend to be large, and ordering too much can lead to wasted food or an overwhelming dining experience.

Jamaican: Respect for elders in Jamaica is similar to the customs in Ethiopia and India. It's common to show great reverence for older individuals, and addressing them as "auntie" or "uncle" is akin to how it's done in South Africa, regardless of familial ties.

Now, let's dive deeper into the values of social relationships and friendship based on firsthand experience. These are simply facts being shared; how they are interpreted or responded to is entirely up to you.

Ethiopia: You can ask any family member to host you if you have no place to stay; it might even be considered obligatory. You might even have to drive them around, take them places, and invite them for certain occasions if short-term stays. It is a responsibility if you know they are in town. Otherwise, it's considered rude, and the whole family and community will know how rude you are.

There may be times when you have to say things you'd rather not say to comfort someone else. Difficult conversations often require a bit of sugarcoating before you get to the point. Your boyfriend or family members might show up at your place unexpectedly—not to spy on you, but to show they care and ensure you're okay.

German: If you're planning to stay with Germans, it's best to keep your visit short—three days max, if possible. You'll need to follow the house rules, and remember; they don't owe you anything. It's a good idea to buy your own food and help with cleaning. Don't expect them to drive you anywhere; you'll need to be independent. Unless you specifically ask for help, they won't offer it, as independence is highly valued—you're not a child. They might not express affection in words but through practical actions that help solve your problems rather than offer emotional comfort. Germans are known for their practicality, not only in their work and engineering but also in how they show up for you in relationships.

South Africa: Easy going and you have small talks everywhere. Mostly, that starts with the problem in the country turning into good friendships and planning get-togethers out of town. They will be there for you anytime you ask for help. Go beyond and above to help you clean up your house and babysit for you, except for any financial or money sacrifices. Money is a serious topic; it does jeopardize or build bonds. If it goes wrong, it might end up with someone getting shot.

Interracial relationships can be challenging. Racism and prejudice are still unresolved issues, and when someone is in a relationship with someone of a different race, they may be viewed as a disgrace by their own community. Unpleasant looks and judgmental stares can be a common experience. How people treat you often depends on your skin color, status, and financial situation.

When you invite a girl out, expect at least three people to show up with her—sometimes even more family members. And in many cases, you'll be expected to cover the cost for everyone. Despite these challenges, it's undeniable that they will show you love and ensure you have a good time.

Japan: In some cultures, direct communication is key, but in Japanese culture, it's essential to explain things in a very polite and considerate manner. This politeness is not quite like the kindness you might see in Ethiopian culture—it's on a whole different level. So, when you're in a mixed family, you constantly have to navigate these differences. It can be emotionally exhausting to learn and unlearn new behaviors every time you change countries or adapt to a new society. However, you've chosen this path, so it's important to stay open-minded and embrace it as the adventure of a lifetime. In the end, it's truly remarkable to learn it all—like learning a new language, but in cultural and social terms rather than just alphabets.

If you grew up in Ethiopian culture in the 80s, where girls were not allowed to speak up in groups, especially in family gatherings where there are adults, you would understand how most young people are unable to articulate their wants and dislikes. Similarly, in most African countries, it was the same for many young men, especially women. If you were shy and didn't say a single word during family gatherings, you were considered well-raised. When guests visit, you are often told to go to your bedrooms. There were norms that boys were not expected to enter the kitchen, while girls were anticipated to serve and provide handwashing with buckets.

Now, suddenly, you would be working with people from the Western world, and you would have to speak up and be bold. Now, you are put in jobs where working in American companies requires you to communicate clearly and directly. For years, many young professionals from Ethiopia struggled to speak up. Sometimes, they are unable to communicate what exactly they want to say or express their business ideas to the big companies — at times creating misunderstanding and being misunderstood. At times, it felt as if they were dismissing us as if we didn't know what we were talking about. The expression in English was difficult to articulate, making it hard to convey what we really wanted to say. You would sit among Polish, Dutch, and German colleagues or friends and can't say anything now since you are tired of being misunderstood. There are times when you're sitting with friends from different countries who have visited Ethiopia, discussing unpleasant things without having the full facts. You may have your own thoughts and explanations ready, but even when you're being insulted, it can be difficult to speak up and share your perspective. Instead, you might find yourself simply smiling and agreeing with everything they say, holding back your opinions.

For some, it takes years to learn how to communicate effectively and stand up for their rights, whether in a crowd or at work. The fear of losing jobs or friendships holds many back, while for others, the same fear prevents them from speaking out. Given the direction the world is heading, it's clear that some old approaches are no longer effective.

Why discuss all these examples and scenarios? Whether you've experienced them firsthand or observed others, you now have a clearer understanding of what it's like. Recognizing and reflecting on these situations is important because it helps you break free from mental constraints and move forward.

It's crucial to challenge and let go of certain outdated norms in order to progress. Hold onto those values that truly matter and serve you, and discard the ones that hold you back. With the global shifts in population movement, there are two key points to emphasize. First, you don't need to rigidly adhere to your culture, norms, or values— choose what works for you and leave behind the dysfunctional ones. Second, cultivating a habit of learning requires an open mind. You need to embrace how things work in different cultures and leverage that knowledge to your advantage. Given the ongoing economic and social changes, intercultural diversity is increasing. Cross-cultural relationships are becoming more common as people unite and form connections. Mixed marriages and multi-ethnic families are no longer rare, and this is the future. The sooner you accept this shift, the sooner you'll find success.

To move forward and thrive, stop resisting change. Embrace new experiences and allow yourself to learn and grow. The foreigners who succeed in Ethiopia are those who make an effort to understand local languages and communicate effectively. Similarly, in South Africa, those who make a lasting impact are the ones who help others without considering race or status. These individuals are resilient, unshaken by challenges, and committed to building a better future. Interracial relationships offer a deeper understanding of people's concerns and needs, giving you a unique advantage in fostering unity. Many people give up and leave the countries where their projects are based because they haven't grasped this yet.

Here's a tip: if you're American and married to a South African living in Cape Town, embrace the local culture. Host a weekend braai and try to learn some of the local language. If your partner is Zulu, make an effort to learn Zulu. Teaching your children the language will be a gift to them, and you'll appreciate it later. The path to your loved ones' hearts and their communities often starts with language.

I know it's not easy, so don't aim for perfection—just do your best. Don't obsess over it! Instead, enjoy the experience and allow your loved ones to enjoy it too.

Core Lesson

Respect and honesty sustain love; temptations and frustrations fade when you commit to balance and understanding.

5

Exploring New Horizons: The Adventures and Uniqueness of Experiences

Get Ready for the unique experience of a lifetime

Many people will tell you that marriage is "hard," sharing stories of their dramas and unfulfilled lives. And it is. It is a lot of work and effort that you need to put into communications, compromises, unselfish actions, etc. Those things in life you work and put your efforts into are those that succeed in giving you joy. While it's understandable to have a viewpoint of "hard," if all you feel is just that, you might be in a dull relationship. Something may be holding you back from fully enjoying the experience of being with your partner. What if you shifted your perspective to: "I am enjoying my husband" or "I am enjoying my boyfriend?" "I am enjoying my wife" or "I am enjoying my girlfriend?" When you approach the relationship as a burden rather than a source of joy, it becomes "harder."

Think back to the times when you were looking for a date—maybe you tried Tinder or another app, or a friend set you up with someone. Remember those days in high school or college when you dressed to impress? The excitement of receiving compliments from your crush, or that moment when someone said, "I love you," or the thrill of your first kiss—these were all part of the journey to something special.

We often overlook the challenges we face to reach the blessing of marriage. Once we achieve it, we sometimes take it for granted instead of celebrating what we once yearned for. You have a partner with whom you can share fun experiences. You are not alone; you can enjoy everything from travel to daily life, including intimacy.

Moreover, this is a unique individual from a different background who is now part of your journey and is a little bit different from what you thought. It's time to adjust your perspective!

Yes, Different challenges have been mentioned in the previous chapters, and there will be more in the future. But for lessons. Hiking the Alps of Switzerland feels scary till you get to do it and experience it. Then you would say, "Wow! I want to do this again next year!" What makes a hiking trip rewarding? What makes the football game you're watching more thrilling? It's the challenges you face along the way—the suspense, the excitement, the heart racing up and down. It's the thrill of it all. It's about confronting those unexpected moments and seeing them through to the end. It's understanding the effort those players put in on the field to earn the trophy. Would it be exciting if you knew it was all fake or performed by robots with preprogrammed moves? No, it's the adventure—the unique experience on every occasion. It's the journey of ups and downs that makes it unforgettable.

Your relationship works the same way. If you're starting a new relationship, don't wish for an easy ride; it will only leave you bored. And if you consider yourself weak, this journey might not be for you. However, if you're ready to embrace the unique experience, you can prepare yourself to thrive in it. All you have to do is believe in your love, your unity, and most of all, in yourself that you can do this.

So, what are all the unique experiences you are talking about?

Growing up, you used to be annoyingly shy, incredibly self-conscious, and a bit geeky. Your sole focus was on your studies and making your parents proud. As "the good kid," you entered University, where you faced crush after crush, unsure of how to handle it. But it was an exciting adventure at the same time, a thing that taught you so much. You might have relished every morning, soaking in the attention, the thrill of making choices, and the anticipation of seeing the guy you secretly liked. You had your first same-culture relationship back in college or high school. Let's just say you discovered how enjoyable it is to be pursued and to go on dates.

You used to be scared of doing things by yourself; scared of traveling alone, hiking big mountains, biking trail adventures and surfing. Not open to trying new foods and languages, missing out on all the beautiful things this world has.

From there, life led you to study abroad and live alone in various countries, where you uncovered just how badass you could be. There's no better lesson than the one you learn through practical life experience. Relationships, communications, and dealing with challenging situations. Also, having had so much fun along the way. Which does not mean you will go through life unscathed or without making mistakes.

If you look back to your own life, sometimes you would chuckle at how vulnerable you once were. Feel proud at the moments when you made things happen for yourself. The days you accomplished something going all in even if you were scared. All these, good and bad, give you a unique experience that helps you appreciate what has been taught. It helps you see what you thought you would never be able to do, but you did it.

Dating within your tribe has its own unique adventures, but dating outside your tribe is a whole lot of different experiences. From the moment you set eyes on someone, you have no idea what surprises await, yet you feel drawn to them. That person is a complete mystery. You're unfamiliar with their language, their food preferences, or how they might react to certain situations. It makes it exciting and stays exciting for years, especially if you like building puzzles.

As you transition from curiosity to reality, you realize you are two distinct individuals. At times, it can feel isolating because the person beside you may not understand you at all. However, you discover your own strength when you choose to understand one another rather than trying to convince them to become like you. In this process of navigating life in a completely different setting, far from your familiar circle, you start to recognize your own capabilities. You discover who you are without attachments — free from the expectations of your parents, culture, favorite foods, or friends — allowing you to define yourself on your own terms. With an endless curiosity every day, another unique thing is happening in the corner.

Cheers to Never Being Boring!

What are some of the most common myths you've heard about marriage and committed relationships? More importantly, what are your own concerns when it comes to intercultural dating and marriage? One common misconception is that long-term relationships eventually become dull. While it's true that not every day will feel like an adventure, you can avoid boredom by actively choosing to keep things exciting. From experiences and those from family and friends observing relationships across various cultures and backgrounds, it's clear that we all share similar human behaviors and experiences. As we move through life, we face relationship challenges in much the same way. So, let's dive into this topic.

Relationships are like a rollercoaster ride; ideally, they should be for your growth and excitement! After all, where's the thrill without a few ups and downs? Without those moments, there wouldn't be a reason to communicate. Arguments can be healthy if you approach them in the right way. When you talk about your arguments or life's challenges, you're addressing the rich variety of backgrounds, beliefs, and cultural norms you each bring to the relationship. These differences add spice to your connection, just like seasoning in a dish.

Now, imagine being in a relationship with someone exactly like you — doing the same things every day, with everything predictable. Would that work? Probably not.

To put it simply, what is agreement without disagreement once in a while? How would you learn about what excites your partner? Does he/she argue with you? Great! That's a positive sign. People who don't care won't bother to argue or make things work. If your partner is arguing with you, take it as a sign that they care and that they're concerned. And you get to experience different types of disagreements and wordings. It can be annoying but never boring!

Viewing Tasks as an Adventure, Not a Burden

In the beginning, it usually is all about having a good time. You date, host house parties, embark on adventures, and gradually introduce him or her to your circle of friends and family. Everything is perfect, yet deep down, you both wonder whether such a relationship can truly last. Every relationship faces doubts, but in cross-cultural relationships, these doubts can stem from unique challenges and perspectives, as mentioned earlier. It's only natural to have concerns and fears about whether the relationship will last—this is a common part of the human experience.

Especially if you're someone who likes to have control or wants to know where things are heading, the uncertainty of a cross-cultural relationship can feel unsettling. You may be someone who needs to know every step of the journey and what the destination will look like. You might find yourself thinking, "We come from completely different cultures, and our dreams seem to be pulling us in different directions." One of you may be willing to make sacrifices for the sake of staying together, while the other is focused on advancing their career. One of you may be unsure about starting a family, and the two of you might not even agree on where to settle or how to shape your future. This leaves you with the dilemma of living in separate countries or trying to make it work in one. Like all relationships, a mixed couple's relationship requires sacrifices, and those choices often come with some tough decisions.

This chapter highlights the importance of fully committing to the required actions from the start. A half-hearted approach—being partially in and partially out—will only lead to more heartache and disappointment, both in your relationships with partners and those around you. By making a clear commitment, you can eliminate doubt and uncertainty, sparing yourself from unnecessary stress and countless days of worry.

Everyone's choice would be to avoid many heartbreaks. Even some of you, the control freaks, do that because you want to avoid getting hurt. You wish to have an easy mind about it all and enjoy life. The doubt and worry just loops you around. It's important to trust the universe, yourselves, and, most importantly, your bond.

The opinions of others only fuelled our doubts. Comments like, "What happens when his contract ends?" "Are you going to live in the US or Kenya?" "What about your own dreams and aspirations?" "Where would you want to buy a house and settle?" "I suggest you buy in Ghana since that's where your family is." "Oh, she's African; she obviously wants to marry you for money," and "Perhaps for a better life," all to contribute to your uncertainty.

When married to an American, some might say, "He's only with her because he wants to go to the US," or "She only married him because she can't find a good man at her age anymore." These comments and opinions will continue to come, and they can slowly drain your spirit, causing you to question a decision you know is loving and right. Over time, doubt can creep in and threaten to break your sense of unity—unless you are fully committed and able to see yourselves as a strong, united team.

Constant doubts from others can lead you to question your bond, making you hesitant to take care of important matters like paperwork, job applications, or buying the home you want. Unfortunately, that's just part of life—no one can ever be completely sure how things will unfold. But the choice is yours: you can choose to commit wholeheartedly and see it as an adventure. Just like achieving success in your studies or business, choose to enjoy the journey and be fully involved. Believing that you can just walk away if things go wrong will rob you of lasting happiness. If you're only halfway in, it's better not to get involved. However, if you're ready to be fully committed to your partner, through both the good and the bad, there are steps you must take, one at a time, to build a solid foundation.

Make a Decision: It's time to choose—are you in or out? Being halfway in, influenced by circumstances or other people's opinions, only leads to frustration and heartbreak for both you and your partner. You need to commit, one way or another.

Visualize Your Unity: Don't just plan—imagine. Picture your life together. What does it look like? Living under one roof? Raising children? Managing challenges? How will you handle arguments, and what will you do as a couple in the years to come? Picture your future as a team.

Communicate with Your Partner: Are you both on the same page? Are your visions for the future aligned? Keep in mind that sacrifices may be necessary. This is about functioning as a unit, not individuals, so be prepared to compromise and adjust to each other's needs.

Act at the Right Time: Trust your instincts — it's clear when the time is right to act. Don't wait. Procrastination only makes things harder, whether it's investing in a shared goal, taking a family trip, handling paperwork, or addressing any other practical matters. Time waits for no one — take action when it counts.

Recognize When Doubt Creeps In: Doubt will arise — whether from outside opinions, disagreements, or feelings within yourself. When it does, pause. Take a step back, look at the facts, and reflect on your shared goals and individual dreams. Identify what needs work, where sacrifices should be made, and what you can let go of to make this relationship stronger.

Put Your Words into Action: Follow through on what you've promised. Taking action as a unit takes time, but it's necessary. When doubt creeps back in, redirect yourself to your vision (Step 2) and act (Step 4). Do the things you agreed on during your conversations (Step 3) and keep moving forward as one.

Again, it's all about perspective. There will be a lot of official things you will be dealing with that you wouldn't face if you just have stayed in your home country and just been married to one. Here's how it goes. You wake up at 3 am and drive to hold a line to renew your ID because they can only serve 300 people daily. It is a long, quiet journey; you arrive, and you are still not sure how it goes. How much you need to pay, and what documents are needed until you are at the door. You leave at the end of the day, finalizing your ID at the last minute, or you will need to come back the next day.

You are moving somewhere with either of the family's side; getting a resident permit is a mission. You have a conference where all the delegates will be there. If you are from a low-income country, there's a chance you might be rejected to come to the country, no matter how important your presence is for the project.

If you ask almost anyone who has been traveling, works with international people, or is married to one, you would hear a lot of frustration with getting paperwork done. However, would you consider it an adventure or a challenge? Some see it as an adventure. But after some time, it becomes the most dreading thing you must do to get things done. Until you come to an understanding that some can be delegated and hire someone who can handle it for you, some would still require your presence, which you have to do. But if you minimize the burden, allowing others to do it for you gets easier.

So, when you are in a country that requires a lot of paperwork to get things done, it's important to delegate. In countries like Ethiopia, the USA, South Africa, Madagascar, India, Thailand, Pakistan, etc., you can find people as agencies or individuals who take those daunting activities off your hands. Then you would be less annoyed being there, save time and have a more joyful experience of the country.

Throughout your life, you'll often find yourself surrounded by officials, foreign staff, and individuals from both higher and middle-class backgrounds. At times, if you're humble enough, you might even spend time with those from lower economic backgrounds. However, in these settings, you'll often encounter people who can drain your energy, as conversations tend to revolve around life's challenges, issues in various countries, and struggles of living in places with their own set of problems. These discussions can sometimes be misunderstood or even seen as beautiful learning experiences. But when the conversation shifts to intercultural differences, tension arises. One person might try to explain why they dislike a certain group, while another expresses frustration over how things are done.

In these situations, a friend may say something in a tone you're not used to, which can lead to offense, arguments, or gossip within the community. The person may then be labeled as rude and become isolated, with no one willing to offer help. This can make you miss social events and even affect your family. A birthday party that should be full of joy might instead leave you with a heavy heart as you struggle to accept that we are all different.

In the midst of dealing with paperwork or official matters, you'll have to choose to view these situations as opportunities rather than obstacles. Your perspective is crucial here. You can either see it as an adventure or as the downside of living in a mixed relationship. When you enter any scenario, ask yourself not, "Why is this happening to me?" but "What am I meant to learn from this? How can I help someone, or what is this experience trying to teach me?" By adopting a mindset focused on growth, adventure, and stepping outside of selfish desires, you'll be able to enjoy the rollercoaster ride of life.

Core Lesson

Every challenge can be an adventure — life feels lighter when you choose joy over burden.

6

The Journey of Your Cross-cultural Love: Lessons, Struggles, and Strengths

Navigating the Pros and Cons

The Benefits

This relationship can become one of the most beautiful chapters of your life. There are moments filled with pure joy, where tears of gratitude and happiness flow freely. You experience the depth of love, the family you've built, and the incredible people you meet along the way. The conversations with your partner, the deep hugs you share with your children, and the unforgettable dinners with strangers who become friends are all because you share the unique bond of being a mixed couple.

There are those intimate coffee chats at campsites that spark new perspectives, the heartwarming sight of your children playing with others in places like Romania or France, where language doesn't matter, and communication is nothing more than gestures and smiles. You may find yourself on a snowboarding trip in the Czech Republic or in a small town like Plauen in Germany, where your kids bond over snowboarding or swimming, communicating only through Google Translate.

And then, there are those magical evenings where you sit down for dinner at a remote campsite with locals who don't speak any English yet share a beautiful evening, connecting through the universal language of laughter, gestures, and the help of a translator app. These moments, filled with warmth and connection, truly redefine what it means to experience life together in a diverse world.

Having a partner with a completely different culture and perspective on life adds a rich layer of adventure to your journey. It challenges you both to learn things you never imagined, sparking creativity and encouraging you to view the world from new angles. It opens the door to loving one another in unique and meaningful ways, expressing affection in ways you might never have expected. As you grow older together, these differences continue to make the experience exciting and ever-evolving.

Watching your children grow, both emotionally and physically, and seeing them develop their own wisdom is a truly beautiful thing. Their kindness, ability to see the world as one, and love for others without judgment are a testament to the power of diversity in shaping their perspectives. They love people for who they are, never undermining or overestimating anyone. It's a remarkable journey, one that allows you to learn from them just as much as they learn from you. It's a beautiful life with a lot of joy and a lot of learning process. It feels like living in a movie, where you're constantly stepping into different dimensions of life, discovering and embracing the unique aspects of existence on this planet. This is especially true if you have a deep passion for exploring various cultures, countries, and languages, each offering its own rich tapestry of experiences. If you're eager to see what lies beyond your community and geographical boundaries, you're embracing the world's vast offerings and selecting what brings you joy and adventure. Simply put, as humans, we are always striving for something better. We aim to be better mothers, improve ourselves, excel in our careers, and develop skills that make us better versions of who we are. Everyone wants a better life—more time with loved ones, a nicer home, better hair, skin, living environments, weather, vacation spots, and so much more. It's an endless pursuit. We all desire better things. Without the drive for improvement, life can feel directionless. This same drive applies to love and personal relationships. Stagnation is something no one desires. Relationships can be incredibly beautiful—the day you met, the first time you saw each other, the moment you introduced your partner to your family — these moments, whether joyful or challenging, build strong, loving connections. While relationships may not always be easy, dating outside your tribe can help you grow into a stronger, more enriched version of yourself, allowing you to experience life from fresh, diverse perspectives.

Dating someone from a different culture and country helps you discover who you truly are. It reveals your strengths and highlights the areas you still need to grow as a person. It teaches you the value of humility. Often, we fall into the belief that our culture, country, relationships, people, and looks are superior to others. Most of us carry this ego to varying degrees. But when you begin to appreciate the beautiful qualities in others, you start to see your own as just one of many. In all the beauty, we cannot ignore the challenges and imperfections, which ultimately help us learn more and deepen our understanding of the person we're getting to know.

The Challenging Aspect

The more you try to understand, the more you realize that you don't have it all figured out. In simple terms, it's a continuous learning process. There's so much to discover about each other, including the origins of your tastes, beliefs, social values, and norms. It requires adjustments and a heads-up, and it can be exhausting. The emotional rollercoaster of being misunderstood and misunderstanding others can feel overwhelming. There will be moments when you feel completely alone on this journey. Just yesterday, everything seemed perfect with your supportive partner, but then, out of nowhere, it feels like you're alone again. And this is just the beginning. As this book delves into the details, hang in there—there are ways to turn these challenges into something positive.

Design Your New Reality

The sooner you detach from the old normal, the sooner you'll find happiness. The hardest part is letting go of what you know—what you're used to and how things were supposed to be. When something new comes your way, it's hard to accept and embrace it. It takes time. But you don't have to stay stuck in the pit of why things aren't the way they used to be. In that space, you might long for things to be as they once were or how you imagined they would be. But that's long gone now. Maybe you're at the very beginning of a new chapter. Regardless, the sooner you accept and design your new normal, the less time you'll waste trying to go back to the old. You have been given something new—it's up to you to surrender to God's good plans and enjoy the journey. I've learned this through tearful and long days that I could have shortened, and I could have saved myself from so many frustrating moments and truly been present to enjoy it all. Looking back, I tell myself, "I wish I knew." So, to save you from wasting your time and energy, learn from me and follow these simple steps as we dive into how to do it.

How to design your new norms

You've come this far in the relationship, so it's going to be your new normal. In fitness, there's a saying: "This is your new normal! This is what you do now." This concept applies to many areas of life, including your relationship.

Just like in fitness, where transforming your body requires changes, things you need to adopt, and things you need to let go of, the same approach works here. I'm going to show you how to apply this step by step in your relationship.

Step one: At first, you might have doubts. When you face inconvenience or insults, those doubts can grow even stronger. Having faith is crucial. It will require you to wake up every day and choose to live beyond what you've known before. New things always demand stepping out in faith. So, the very first step is to decide that you're in it 100%. No one foot in, one foot out. It's not an exaggeration to say you can't do it right or be happy if you don't. It will take your energy and unwavering love to stand by your new journey.

Step two: Let go of your old ways of thinking and reacting. In the beginning, it won't be easy, but with practice and self-discipline, you can train yourself to pivot when your old habits try to take over. For example, let's say your partner is Italian and you're Ethiopian. He yells at you for something you did that he didn't want you to do. Your initial reaction might be to think he's being racist and bring up the history between Ethiopians and Italians. Suddenly, what could've been just a simple disagreement becomes about history, nationality, and race. This is the moment where you need to pivot your thoughts. Take a deep breath and train your mind to address the problem at hand, not something else. This brings us to the next step: implanting the new you.

Step three: The new version of you is taking root. With practice and the lessons learned from step two, your mind and body are beginning to adopt this new way of thinking, speaking, and acting. The more you continue, even if you slip up occasionally, the new normal will eventually become second nature. It will be deeply rooted. You'll start to see situations differently. For example, you might wonder why someone assumed something was done out of racism or entitlement when, in reality, it was just a logical argument.

Step four: Your new normal is now well established. At this stage, it's about nurturing and protecting it from anything hindering its growth. Just like a tree or plant, no matter how strong and deeply rooted it becomes, external forces will occasionally try to shake it. Similar to grass, there might be things that pretend to support its growth but actually drain its energy, blocking the sunlight.

It's like when someone is trying to quit alcohol or drugs. They might return to those same circles once, then again, and before they know it, they're back at square one. Be cautious. Don't put yourself in that situation until you're strong enough to handle it. Once you are in those environments, limit your time there. Most importantly, don't listen to or agree with things that go against your values. Stay firm in your beliefs.

Step five: Share your new normal with those around you. You are still the same person but have a different approach to life and relationships. You now hold yourself and others to a new standard. If others can't meet that standard or disagree, calmly explain where you stand and embrace the acceptance of each other's differences. This new normal is about tolerance and accepting your partner for who they are, not where they come from. This new normal is about no longer seeking love, understanding, and acceptance in places, things, or people that don't meet your standards. This new normal has no expectations or rejections based on your differences. Instead, it's about making intentional decisions and acknowledging that everyone approaches life with their own unique priorities and perspectives.

This is your new normal now. You are in a relationship with your new partner from a different country. Here are a few examples of the training categories in the new normal.

Muscle: Your relationship is strong and can handle heavy lifting, and punches that are through at you!

Endurance: without breaking down, you endure daily life issues without injuring your relationship.

Agility and stamina: You have trained now to stretch your joints and train your muscles. You can run longer and at the required pace without feeling easily exhausted. The long-term commitment doesn't scare you. Rather, you will start to enjoy this relationship in the long run.

Discipline: Constantly staying in peace and doing the right things as they come has become easier. Life is more enjoyable and breathable.

You look sexy & healthy: You guys are looking amazing with your healthy relationships. The way you are for each other, the way you talk, everything about you looks hot!

Confronting Prejudice: No Longer Ignorable

You've navigated the various phases of dating and have now entered a committed relationship. Every relationship involves its own compromises and wonderful benefits. However, you can't dismiss the thoughts and experiences that people will throw at you over the years. This book aims to provide you with both the good and the bad, preparing you for the battles you will face and helping you enjoy your life choices.

In training—whether in fitness or yoga—physical capabilities are closely tied to the mind and the thoughts you entertain. These thoughts can either hinder or motivate you. The same principle applies here. The world will challenge you, and it's crucial to know how to protect your goals and win the match.

One of the heaviest burdens you may face is confronting prejudice. This isn't just about the prejudice you encounter in the wider world; it becomes a deeply personal challenge in your own life. You'll visit relatives and go to places where only Black people gather. At family dinners, you may find yourself as the only Black individual among a group of Caucasians. While shopping, one partner might be scrutinized while the other is treated with respect and dignity. Your mixed children may be well-received in one community but regarded as inferior in another. A minor disagreement can suddenly escalate into racial discrimination, causing tensions to rise and contexts to be lost.

You will encounter these challenges in every aspect of your life. You might find yourself in training rooms where no other people of color are present, becoming an example of stereotypes related to poverty or colonization. This experience can be exhausting and inescapable, regardless of your life choices. If you choose this path, be prepared to develop a thick skin, cultivate inner peace, and build mental strength.

You'll find yourself in situations where people ask, "Can I touch your hair?" or, when you straighten your hair, they'll say, "Now you look beautiful, like an Indian." You'll be left wondering whether to take these comments as compliments or if they're microaggressions in disguise.

So, listen closely: whether you come from a low-income or undeveloped country or a wealthier nation, pay attention to the upcoming chapters. It's time we normalize humanity, knowledge, understanding, clarity, and unity.

Ethnic Bais in Your Lives

The common assumption is that the person from a higher-income country is the "good" partner, while the other is seen as the "charity" case. Those you meet—whether acquaintances, friends, or complete strangers—often have no understanding of who you are as a couple. They don't know your background, what you do, or what your beliefs are. Instead, they see you and attempt to fit you into predefined categories, making conclusions based on limited information.

When facing this kind of racial bias, it's best to keep things simple. Let people think whatever they want; it's beyond your control, whether you're a mixed couple or not. Why waste your energy trying to change someone else's opinion? Ask yourself: Does it really matter if they know the facts? You might never encounter them again. Why give a second of your life to someone who doesn't care about you and contributes nothing to your experience?

It takes time, but train your mind to let go of these negative thoughts. Carrying around this mental baggage is like holding onto trash that stinks up your life. So, dispose of it where it belongs and move through life with open arms, ready to embrace only the good and new experiences that come your way.

Unfairness and Prejudice in the Relationship

There can be a tendency to make assumptions about your partner, especially during heated conversations. Your mind often reverts to negative stories you've heard about a particular race, triggering memories or anecdotes from the past. For example, when you would get upset with your partner, he might recall that Ethiopian girls are often labeled as "drama queens." At that moment, instead of addressing your concerns, he might interpret your complaints through that stereotype rather than understanding the issues you are genuinely trying to address.

Consider a situation where your partner is from the UK, and you are from Kenya. You know, deep down, that this person loves you, but during discussions, he may interrupt you or make a comment in front of friends that feels dismissive of your Kenyan heritage. You might perceive his words as undermining your community and your identity, which could lead you to view the conversation through that lens. If you're perceptive enough, you might snap out of this mindset; others, however, may linger in it, developing resentment toward the race as a whole.

You're sitting at a fancy restaurant in Germany on your first date. As the waiter pours chilled white wine into your glass, you pick it up, holding it by the stem to smell and taste it. Suddenly, everyone's eyes are on you. Your German date looks at you in disbelief and says, "That's not how you hold a white wine glass; that's embarrassing," as she ducks her head in shame. The waiter and others in the restaurant exchange glances, shaking their heads in silent judgment. Truth be told, no one cares how you hold your wine or whiskey glass as long as you're enjoying the company, especially in an African context. But, of course, that's a whole different culture.

You're sitting with your aunts, mom's friends, and other relatives just three days before your wedding. Everyone is excited and busy preparing for the big day, ensuring everything goes smoothly. Your fiancé is a handsome, intelligent Black American man, and you're madly in love with him. You can't wait for everyone to meet him. Suddenly, one woman in the group says, "I hope your kids don't get your husband's nose. It'd be better if they looked more Ethiopian, like you, than like him," and they all laugh. She says nothing in return, respecting the tradition of not speaking back to elders. But the comment hits her deeply, leaving her feeling sad and regretful, questioning why they had to fly all the way to Ethiopia for the wedding in the first place.

Even now, years later, she reflects on the hurt and wishes she had said something to that woman. How could someone from her own background, an African woman herself, insult her fiancé in front of so many people? The incident left a long-lasting wound that she's never discussed with her family. It's a painful reality, one many face but rarely talk about.

In intercultural and interracial relationships, misunderstandings can quickly escalate into arguments or even major conflicts. What should be a peaceful evening may end in a quarrel, and trips that are meant to be joyful can turn into moments of making one person feel inferior and the other unwelcome. Instead of creating cherished memories, these situations leave wounds and scars. So, how can you prevent this from happening? How do you keep the love alive without allowing resentment to build?

The first step is to free your mind. Clear out all the preconceived notions and negative judgments you've absorbed about that specific race. Let go of the stereotypes and biases you've heard from the media, stories, or historical narratives. Begin seeing your partner as an individual, not as a representative of their country or culture. Once you shed the biased lenses shaped by past influences, allow yourself to truly get to know your partner for who they are. Avoid filtering them through preconceived notions—approach them with an open mind. Stay focused on the present and gently steer the conversation away from old biases, always bringing it back to the here and now.

Prejudices Within Relatives and Close Family Members

For many family members, making racially offensive remarks comes naturally, often without even realizing it. It can be difficult for them to understand what is wrong with their words and actions. While you tend to notice macro-level racism, the microaggressions often go unnoticed at first, only to resurface later with thoughts like, "Wait, what did they mean by that?"

Friends and family may sometimes make racist comments or cross-cultural jokes—often unintentionally. These can range from remarks about hair, skin color, or eating habits to how food is prepared or consumed. There are many layers to consider. Interestingly, people from non-colonized countries often struggle to recognize these cues or understand their significance in today's context. Some may be aware of the offense but feel it's acceptable to speak this way because of their close relationship with you. Others may project their own negative experiences or stories they've heard from others onto you. Regardless of the intention, microaggressions and racism can deeply affect you, your partner, and your children.

While you may encounter biased comments and actions from strangers, addressing insults and remarks from family members can be far more challenging. For those new to intercultural relationships or navigating interracial communication for the first time, it can be difficult to recognize these issues and know how to handle them. This book will provide you with everything you need to understand. It will help you navigate the unique position your relationship may place you in and the journey you'll go through. Everyone should know these insights or have someone share them before facing the challenges that come with intercultural love. This love brings not only exciting and beautiful moments but also tough lessons that will make you stronger. With this knowledge, many could have avoided separation, better understood the complexities involved, and saved themselves from fractured family relationships and the heartbreak of mixed-race children facing difficult situations.

Throughout this journey, you'll experience significant personal growth, learning, and evolving with every step. However, one of the most challenging aspects of this growth is developing tolerance, especially when faced with the difficult challenge of dealing with racism from family members.

Now, let's explore a step-by-step guide on how to address these discrepancies early on before they evolve into deeply held beliefs that affect your mindset and well-being.

Number One: Breathe!

The key lies in your breath. I'm not sure what works best for you—whether it's walking away, closing your eyes, or using another technique—but take a deep breath, inhale and exhale to avoid saying something you'll regret or getting emotionally caught up in the moment. Try to position yourself as an observer, witnessing the situation rather than getting lost in feelings of betrayal.

Treat the situation as if it were an object. Set it aside and deal with it without internalizing it as part of you. Think of it this way: if the wind blows through an open window and knocks over your favorite picture frame, are you going to cry and say, "How could the wind do this to me? I'm so hurt"? I hope not. Instead, see it as an incident. You can either repair it, if possible, or replace it and move on. Life continues.

Treat incidents with family members and friends the same way — simply as incidents. Address the issue and try to fix it, making it clear that racial comments are unacceptable. Set clear boundaries and communicate them effectively.

You may need to address these issues a few times, but if the behavior continues, it might be necessary to step back from the relationship for your mental well-being. In those cases, limit your time with that person and keep interactions brief.

Number Two: Be Mindful!

Mindfulness isn't just about being aware of our own actions — it's also about being conscious of our surroundings and the relationships we have, as they play a crucial role in our well-being. Being mindful of friends and family is key to maintaining happiness in your relationships.

Often, we overlook certain issues, thinking they aren't important just because they involve relatives. We might avoid addressing them to avoid being seen as overly sensitive. However, when these behaviors go unaddressed, they can escalate into bigger problems that are harder to resolve, eventually leading to resentment.

It's important to stay aware of the actions of those around us without being overly critical. I'm not suggesting you become picky, but I encourage you to pay attention to what people say and do. When someone makes a comment, ask for clarification. Confront situations directly instead of making assumptions. If needed, educate others and set healthy boundaries.

Start by simply asking, "I want to understand what you mean. Can you clarify that?" Approach these conversations with curiosity and a genuine desire for clarity.

Number Three: Let Go.

You've likely heard the phrase "Let go" countless times, but we all know it's easier said than done. The good news is, with practice, you can train both your mind and your actions. At first, it may feel uncomfortable—just like the resistance you feel when starting a new workout routine. But consistently choosing what's right over what's easy will eventually become second nature, much like adopting a healthy lifestyle.

You work out, eat well, and then you let go. You've made the right decisions; now it's time to let things unfold naturally. After taking those initial steps, release the situation and trust that the universe will handle the rest as you move forward. Simply put, practice letting go. When someone says or does something that triggers you, take a moment to step back, mentally and emotionally. Imagine it as someone handing you a bag of smelly trash to bring into your house—your inner space and heart. Would you accept it, or would you refuse to take it in the first place? Even if you accidentally took it, once you realize it serves no purpose for you, you let it go, right? Just like that, when you decide you don't need that "trash" in your life, you let it go or throw it away. This is how you train and strengthen your willpower and mindset.

Confronting Prejudice in Children

Over 50% of young children struggle to understand their relationships with peers. Kids create their own lives and social circles, and their experiences in these spaces can either empower or hurt them. Every interaction—whether a simple comment or a more noticeable incident—plays a part in shaping their identity, influencing how they speak, behave, and even develop preferences for certain foods.

Even questions that may seem innocent, like "How do you wash your hair?" can spark strong emotions. It's vital to educate our children about these dynamics. Racism can appear in children's lives in more overt ways than it does in adults, and young children often don't know how to process or handle these experiences.

Number One: Be Open with Them

It's better they hear it from you than from the world. From age 5-6, they sense and can understand when you bring the conversation to their level of understanding and explain in the ways they perceive as education. Choose to educate them and not cover up when incidents happen. Don't change the subject when they ask you questions. Avoiding conversations about how the world might treat them isn't protective; in fact, it can be harmful if you don't prepare them. You don't need to have a serious sit-down talk — casual moments work best. You can bring it up while driving them to school, during pick-up, or while cooking together. Talk about things like friends, school, or family in simple, age-appropriate terms they can understand. Keep the conversation informative and clear.

Number Two: Be Mindful of How You Handle Situations

Teaching your children how to confront situations is important, but they learn best from observing your actions. What they see you do is more impactful than any theoretical lesson; it stays in their minds for life. Therefore, it's crucial to be mindful of how you respond in front of them.

School incidents happen. Not just the child but you as a parent would have a heated encounter where one would be shouted at if someone from a different race or country — say, an Italian — were to speak loudly and in a belittling manner to an Ethiopian parent, Given the historical tensions between Ethiopians and Italians, all the racial experiences in Europe flood back, leaving many parents shaken of their identity, self-worth, and respect. Fortunately, lessons and experiences teach you to respond logically instead of resorting to loud arguments. But when you are new to such new situations, it's a different story. You might fight, cry, hide in the bathroom, panic, or start worrying about how your child is going to make it in this world.

There are times when you may feel like you're losing control, unsure of how to respond or behave. You and your children might face microaggressions, even within Africa itself. Sometimes, it's African to African or European to European, simply because someone is from a different country. Unfortunately, that's the reality. But change is possible—and don't overlook the small changes. These small efforts are the building blocks of the larger transformations we all want to see in the world.

Living in a predominantly white neighborhood often exposes you to subtle comments and actions. For example, one day, as you're leaving a supermarket you've been shopping at for years, you might experience a black security guard wanting to check your bag or follow you around the store—especially if you're not dressed up for shopping. So, how do you help your children? Simply put, by showing them how it's done. That's why you need to read through to understand how to navigate this mixed culture life.

Number Three: Mastering Focus on Self

One of the most important aspects of a child's development is helping them understand who they are, embracing their roots, accepting what they cannot change, and appreciating the fact that they are wonderfully created and loved. It's our responsibility to continually remind them, guiding their growing minds to become strong, confident, and productive individuals.

Challenges are a vital part of this process. Just as we train young athletes to be both physically and mentally prepared, we should do the same for our children. By helping them master their skills and embrace their uniqueness, we guide them on the path the universe has specifically set for them.

The Importance of Learning and Teaching

Teach Your Partner, Don't Argue

Often, we take our frustrations out on our partners instead of addressing the main issues. Teaching an adult can be daunting, especially after years of being together. You might wonder, "Why can't they figure this out on their own?" The truth is, sometimes there are lessons that need to come from you rather than from others. Ultimately, it's about communication and establishing a common ground of understanding.

No one else can establish that understanding but the two of you; it's something that only you can nurture together. No one is more aware of your situation than you and your partner. It's crucial to sort out your own feelings and learn how to teach each other about your differences — what is acceptable and what isn't, as well as anything that could lead to misunderstandings.

Stay Calm. When emotions run high and thoughts like "How could you?" arise, take a moment to walk away or breathe before responding. It's important to approach the situation thoughtfully rather than reactively.

Use a Respectful Tone. Your tone matters greatly when conveying your message. Aim to communicate respectfully; a single instance of disrespect can lead to resentment, ultimately eroding the respect you have for one another.

Express Your Feelings. Share your perspective and how you feel, rather than assuming how your partner perceives the situation or how they should feel about it.

Postpone the Discussion if Necessary. Delaying the conversation can be beneficial. Giving yourselves time allows for a more realistic, reasonable, and logical discussion, making it easier to find common ground.

Avoid Public Confrontations. Whether it's in front of your kids or family members, try not to involve them in your disputes. Doing so can lead to feelings of misunderstanding and division. Additionally, it can be challenging to return to a loving state in front of family once tensions rise. Remember, this is your relationship and your issue; keep it between the two of you.

Allow Your Partner to Be a Student

Navigating family dynamics can be tricky, whether you like it or not. Communication styles, behavior, and cultural differences often create tension. When you take your relationship to the next level, introducing each other's families can bring about some awkward moments. In cultures like Ethiopian, for example, it's common for guests to have food continuously piled onto their plates, even after they've said they're full. It's a sign of love, hospitality, and a warm welcome — to eat, drink, and enjoy.

However, in other cultures, like German culture, family gatherings typically involve serving oneself and finishing what's on the plate. Here, the host doesn't usually anticipate when someone's plate is empty, and additional servings aren't automatically offered. This is when you may find yourself needing to gently pull your mom aside and explain that this practice isn't typical in German culture.

Though it may seem like a small issue, it's important to remember that these differences can be confusing for older family members to understand. It's up to the couple to foster mutual understanding, respect each other's backgrounds, and approach these situations with patience and openness. Educating each other about cultural nuances, tolerances, and expectations is where learning and growth happen.

Mastering How to Deal with Rejection

History shows that humans often have a natural skepticism when faced with the unfamiliar, whether it's new technology, methods, or even life changes. This skepticism is common, whether it's about vaccines or emerging innovations. When something new is introduced, especially if you're among the first to embrace it, you may encounter resistance and verbal criticism from your community, family, or even new friends and relatives.

While constructive criticism is necessary for growth, both individually and as a couple, it can be difficult not to feel rejected at times. Seeking love and acceptance is already challenging enough, and when that rejection comes from people you expect to support you, it can sting. As an African, for example, you may notice that when you enter a store with your partner, they are treated more favorably while you are met with suspicion, almost as if you're automatically assumed to be a thief. This can happen at border controls, in restaurants, or even within your own family, where you may feel invisible, underappreciated, or simply given a perfunctory "thanks for coming." These moments can be deeply hurtful.

Be Free and Own Your Tribe: It's Special

One common mistake we often make is spending years trying to fit in. We feel the need to explain our choices and those of our partners to others, only to find that they still don't understand. We tend to seek comfort in the people and culture we grew up with, believing that's where we truly belong. But over time, both you and they evolve. You've left your community and formed a life with your partner, and now they are your family. As the saying goes, "Therefore, a man shall leave his father and his mother and hold fast to his wife, and they shall become one flesh." This truth is something we witness time and again.

Now, you are in the process of creating your own tribe — whether it's interracial, intercultural, married, or single. It's important to embrace the opportunity to build something new with the gifts life has given you.

Many of you hold on too tightly to our old tribes, trying to make relationships work despite conflicting beliefs. This can lead to feelings of rejection from the very community that raised you. The reality is that they may not know how to process or categorize your decisions or how to adapt to the changes in your life. Don't take it personally. They might expect you to stay the same person you were when you left, just as you may expect them to understand you simply because you share a common background. Sound familiar?

When you notice this dynamic, stop exhausting yourself and trying to fit in. While it's important to maintain relationships with family and friends, understand that your true sense of belonging lies with the person you have chosen to share your life with—your partner.

Helping Couples Navigate the Unique Dynamics

You're in a mixed-race or mixed-culture relationship, or perhaps you work with colleagues from a completely different culture and country. As you spend more time together and get to know each other better, you might begin to find yourself becoming more critical of the way they do things, their actions, or even their behavior. This isn't necessarily in a negative way—it's just different from what you're used to or familiar with. Instead of trying to understand and embrace these differences, you might find yourself labeling or judging them. This doesn't only happen in interracial marriages but also in relationships where people come from different countries within the same race. For example, when someone from Germany marries a Dutch person, it's interesting to see how they often focus on their differences rather than what they have in common.

Ethnic bias and division aren't limited to any one group, including white couples. While it might be hard for some to accept, even they can hold prejudiced views. Racism can exist within African countries, between different African nations, or even among European countries, where many are openly critical of each other, often viewing some as lesser. When it comes to people of color, racism may appear as subtle politeness or, in some cases, more overt hostility. In these situations, humor can offer a much-needed escape from the weight of anger and frustration. The prejudices adults express at home often show up in schools and society as children absorb and mimic the behaviors and attitudes they learn from their caregivers. They react to situations based on the lessons they've been taught and the examples set for them.

A friend who perfectly embodies the stereotypical German girl—her culture, style, adventurous spirit, and demeanor. She's married to an upper-class South African man who is equally quintessentially Afrikaans. His accent and the way he refers to "these people" when talking about Black individuals often carry a negative tone. As a Black person, being around them at a barbecue (or "braai") can be uncomfortable. When he uses the term "black people," it's often clear that he's only referring to South African Black people, and it can be quite offensive. In relationships like this, where there's an underlying disrespect for non-white people, it almost seems like a match made in heaven. When people share a common prejudice, it can foster a sense of unity among them. Individually, people may be pleasant, but in a group setting, their dynamics can be overwhelming. You might enjoy spending time with someone one-on-one, but when the group is homogenous—whether entirely white or entirely black—the way they handle differing opinions can be uncomfortable. Families often overlook that the children in these environments are absorbing these conversations and attitudes. Observing how kids interact on the playground shows how adult conversations influence their behavior. What they hear at family gatherings or weekend get-togethers shapes their understanding of how they should behave. Children internalize these discussions and start to believe that's how they should act. Being mindful of what you, the adults, say and do in front of children is crucial in creating a future that values unity and understanding.

So, sitting on this beautiful balcony enjoying the fine wines of South Africa, then having their fancy whisky. And the husband just taps on her and says, "She is not flat like the Germans; she actually has an African ass," And you would be like, umm, what is that supposed to be now. The Germans don't have one, or you're acting like those Deutch slave owners and slapping on my lady's ass in front of everyone here. As someone listening to this, it is hard not to react at that moment; instead simply smiles and says nothing as a black person sitting there watching and listening to this nonsense. South African whites, particularly Afrikans, have a reputation for certain behaviors, including heavy drinking, which can lead to issues like alcoholism. This stereotype not only influences the social gatherings but also impacts their relationships significantly. If you have been there, you may have noticed how honest conversations go over drinks with locals. Either way, things get uncomfortable even within the same race, and it then again becomes a situation of cross-cultural relations.

While it can be uncomfortable to experience or witness societal judgment and stereotypes, all we can really do is be human and show grace to others. We're not in a position to lay down strict rules like the Ten Commandments — what may be right for one person can be wrong for another. The key is not making others feel unwelcome, inadequate, or like they can't cope with life's challenges. Instead, embrace them and strive to be as kind and accepting as possible, celebrating the differences they bring.

Remember, the way we act, respond to situations, and speak about others will shape how our children behave in the world. They are watching us and learning from our actions. The way they interact with the world and treat others is influenced by what they observe. So, ask yourself: What are you teaching those around you and the next generation? As someone from a mixed family, I find it crucial to teach the value of unity, not division. Perfection is not required — what matters is making the best effort we can with the knowledge we have. That alone is enough.

Core Lesson

Love across cultures is stronger when you design your own norms and face prejudice with courage.

7

Guiding Pathways: Empowering Parents, Communities, and Schools

Empowering Parents to Support cross-cultural Couples and Mixed-Race Children

On any given Saturday, you might find yourself picking up your grandchild from your son's house, planning to take her to the park for a fun, uneventful day, confident everything will go as expected. Your granddaughter, who is half-Japanese and half-South African, loves playing at her favorite playground. But when you arrive, the nanny at the gate informs you that the playground is full and you can't enter. What you don't realize, though, is that the playground has a policy that rejects black or mixed-race children. Confused and upset, you call your son's partner, your daughter-in-law. She quickly understands the situation, recognizing the deeply ingrained prejudice in the community, and in a panic, rushes to the park, creating a scene. Now you're left wondering: who is at fault here? How do you explain this situation to your 5-year-old granddaughter? As a grandmother to a mixed-race child, what should you have known or done differently? How well do you understand the challenges your son and daughter-in-law face? Are you equipped to support them and teach your granddaughter how to navigate the complexities of her mixed heritage? These are the tough questions that demand both empathy and communication skills in order to create a safe, supportive environment for your granddaughter.

Another common issue is that families of interracial couples often place high expectations on these individuals, which can create pressure on the relationship and, in turn, impact the couple's life and their children. It can be particularly challenging to explain the importance of stepping back if they don't know how to support in a way that ensures safety and ease for everyone involved. A lack of clear communication and understanding can lead to a sense of separation between the couple and their families. The couple may feel isolated, while the parents may feel unwelcome in the couple's home. Over time, this tension can cause both sides to become reluctant to reach out, even when help is needed.

Embracing Diversity and Overcoming Challenges

When you start dating someone from a different race or country, the first thing that often comes to mind is whether your family will accept them. Beyond societal pressure, the way parents react can vary greatly. In some cases, parents are supportive as long as the couple treats each other well, but they often have many questions. There is also the added pressure of how to respond to society's expectations. Many young couples focus solely on their new relationship, often forgetting the strain and confusion it can create within the family. Unlike in the Western world, growing up in a culturally conservative society can raise many questions about accepting interracial marriage. Parents who have traveled and are more liberal may be more accepting, while others may be more traditional, requiring considerable effort to reach an understanding. Some parents will meet halfway, continuing the relationship with their kids and grandkids, even if it feels uncomfortable. Regardless, for many, it's an ongoing process of learning. Often, both the couple and the parents only realize what they should have understood earlier after significant emotional damage is done, making it harder to heal broken hearts. This chapter aims to guide you through navigating these challenges, helping you overcome them before anyone gets hurt. It's about understanding what could have saved you from heartache, tough conversations, and disappointment—before it's too late to teach your granddaughter or son the lessons they need from you and to avoid future regrets.

Before diving into specific scenarios and solutions, it's important to understand some basic challenges you may face as the parent of a mixed-race couple. One of the first things that might come to your mind is questioning why your child is with this person. At first, it may not feel genuine, and it takes time to truly get to know the partner. This process will unfold over time, as discussed in Chapter 3.

Another challenge is the feeling of being uninvited or distanced, especially when you feel the need to call ahead and confirm plans. This hesitation can make you reluctant to offer help or support when the couple needs it, creating an emotional gap. Over time, this can lead to further separation from your own child, complicating the relationship and making it harder to navigate. For example, when inviting them for the holidays, you may struggle with how to communicate the invitation properly. In most African cultures, simply serving food on the table isn't enough—you are expected to go around and offer more sauce or refill your guest's plate, even if they refuse. In fact, leaving food on the plate is a sign of being very full. However, in some European cultures, this would be considered pushy. In this setting, guests are expected to serve themselves, and finishing everything on the plate is considered polite. Both sides may end up feeling confused about the "right" way to host, adding further complexity to their cultural differences.

A common mistake in communication within mixed-couple families is expressing love and respect in ways that reflect one's own preferences rather than considering how the couple might want to receive love. This is why self-education is important. While this approach may feel natural or exciting in the early stages of a relationship, it can later come across as thoughtless or dismissive—essentially sending the message, "I don't care; I tried." To maintain a loving and healthy relationship over time, it's important to understand and adapt to each other's love languages. This situation places a significant emotional toll on the couple, the grandparents, and the children involved.

It's heartbreaking when you express love or offer a welcoming gesture, believing you're showing care, only for it to go unappreciated by the other person. The same applies to the couple involved—understanding the love language of the parents is essential. However, it's not about forcing what you believe they should like; it's about learning what the new normal looks like. It's about making an effort to understand and embrace inclusivity, regardless of the different choices they make. Unconditional love can be difficult to offer, but the feeling of being unwanted or excluded is especially painful when it comes from someone you trusted to always have your back. When you've entrusted someone with the responsibility to love and accept you, no matter how you choose to live or who you marry, it's devastating when that support is not felt. Everyone has their own way of feeling valued, and when those needs aren't met, it can lead to feelings of neglect or disconnection. Recognizing and respecting each other's love language is key to ensuring that gestures of love are meaningful and strengthen relationships.

When you're invited to an African home, you might find only traditional dishes on the buffet. If you attend a European gathering, the options might be limited to various breads with toppings, ham, potato salad, and some sliced fruits and vegetables. Come on, we need our meat! And by "meat," I mean chicken or beef — let's skip the pork if possible. The same goes for those married to someone Japanese; make an effort to include noodles or sushi, and at the very least, provide chopsticks. Be considerate and thoughtful to maintain a beautiful relationship. These are the simplest things mixed couples and families are sensitive about, and it all comes down to making those small efforts and clear, productive conversations.

When you show respect, warmth, or love, it's important for the host to acknowledge and appreciate your efforts. There's nothing more frustrating than repeatedly explaining something, only to realize the other person hasn't understood or taken anything from it. And still do the same. Another challenge for parents of mixed-race couples is communication. Not knowing how to — not knowing when to pass the message or ask questions since it comes with questioning it again and again if you should. This is why the tips below will help you.

Here are a couple of things that would smoothen and maintain your relationship with your grandkid and the interracial couple:

1. **Communicate clearly from the start.** The transition from dating days to a serious relationship and marriage becomes smoother over time only if you communicate clearly from the beginning on. This includes having open, sometimes uncomfortable conversations about race, financial status, and living arrangements (whether living in the same country or being far apart). Addressing these topics early helps prepare both the couple and the family emotionally, fostering understanding and reducing potential stress later on.

2. **Stop avoiding the cross-county conversations.** Recognize the cultural differences, racial biases, and challenges that come with raising mixed couples and mixed-race children. Educating yourself about intercultural relationships and the partner's country norms, culture, history, food, and social values will help you connect not just with your child's partner but with all the in-laws. This builds unity and strengthens family connections.

3. **Be mindful that the children are observing and learning from you.** You have the opportunity to teach them life values and wisdom that they might not learn otherwise — such as history, language, culture, ethics, respect, and kindness. If they

observe the good, they implement the good; if bad, that will stick in bad ways from an early age. When, as parents, you don't have the time or wisdom to impart these lessons, you seek guidance.

4. *Create a safe space for emotional support.* A space where speaking up is safe to prevent feelings of isolation and not belonging. Avoid covering up emotions or pretending everything is fine when something is hurtful. Addressing issues directly, confronting them, and putting them on the table is the only way to heal and deepen relationships.

5. **Make your first line of communication your own child not the partner**. The communication channels and ways of conveying messages between these two individuals can be complex and sometimes misunderstood. It's better to consult with your child before involving their partner in the conversation.

6. **Don't be afraid to be there for your son or daughter**. They need you, even if they don't say it. Check in on them occasionally and ask for their help when you need it. Assumptions can erode love, unity, and support—things you both need from each other. Focus on understanding, active listening, and acknowledging each other's feelings and perspectives.

7. **Expect that this relationship will be different from the ones you've known before**. Unless you

are spending more time together, some things might even be misunderstood, such as wording and ways of saying things. The other side of the grandparents might have taught them the way of doing certain things, but now you are telling them to do things in another way. You tell them to believe in one thing, and the other side of the family tells them to believe in another, potentially discarding what you are trying to genuinely teach your grandkids. Remember not to create extra confusion, but keeping an open mind is essential to avoid heartbreak.

8. **Be clear about your wants and boundaries.** After years of living in a mixed-cultural environment, the child you once knew will evolve. Living in a different country often leads to adopting a new lifestyle. It's important to remember that they are still your child, and you shouldn't question their love or respect for you. Recognize that as they grow and experience new things, they will change. Embrace the new person they've become, and don't expect them to be the same as before.

9. **Defend your children against extended family members.** Don't focus on what others might say; focus on your child's well-being. Recognize that relatives, colleagues, friends, and neighbors may have opinions—both good and bad—but don't let

those affect your relationship. Stay true to your principles and ignore ignorance.

10. **Don't be afraid to ask to see your grandchildren.** Sometimes, couples may feel hesitant or unsure about letting you take them for a sleepover, ice cream, or to the park. Make your desire known without fear.

11. **Don't make assumptions—ask for clarification.** When you have questions or doubts, it's best to ask for a clear answer. If you want to teach your grandchildren something or take them somewhere, communicate beforehand. This includes decisions like ear piercings, hair dyeing, or trips to the playground.

Mixed Couple Towards Their Parents

One summer in Italy, a couple—an Italian man married to a German woman—spent the day at the beach with their kids. Afterward, the couple spontaneously decided to visit his Italian grandparents. While driving there, the wife grew visibly uncomfortable and stressed about the idea. Upon arriving, the grandparents weren't outside. The family's property was large, and the grandparents were probably inside, staying cool to avoid the extreme heat.

Suddenly, the wife became upset, expressing her frustration that the visit wasn't planned in advance. She argued that showing up unannounced—especially with guests—was inconsiderate, and a proper conversation should have taken place beforehand. The husband, excited to introduce his friends and children to his parents, was disappointed, but the wife stood firm, and they left after a brief discussion without visiting.

In both Italian and Ethiopian cultures, it's common for people to visit relatives unannounced, especially on weekends, and the surprise is often well received; people are generally happy to enjoy a casual coffee or a glass of wine together. However, not everyone is comfortable with surprises; some parents may find them unsettling. A little heads-up or prior communication can help avoid discomfort and ensure everyone feels heard and respected.

As grandparents, it's especially important not to impose changes on them simply because they don't align with your personal preferences as a couple. While you may have your own ways of doing things, it's essential to recognize that your parents and grandparents have lived lives full of experiences that shaped their values. Trying to impose your way of doing things can create friction, and it's crucial to appreciate the wisdom they have to offer.

When bringing someone from a different country into your life, it can feel like a huge shift for your parents and relatives. It's often best to introduce the idea gradually rather than springing it on them all at once, especially if it is someone from a completely different race. In the beginning, you may feel anxious about how they will react, but remember that if they truly love you, they'll ultimately be happy for you. Their primary concern will likely be whether your partner is a good fit for you, and as long as you are clear and honest with them, they'll respect your decision. If they disapprove, you'll have to accept the consequences, but remember: this is your life and your choice.

It's important to have open discussions about cultural differences and relationships early on—preferably during the dating phase—rather than waiting until after marriage. In some cultures, like Ethiopia, children might feel reluctant or even fearful about sharing their dating lives with their parents, which can lead to distance between family members. Being transparent from the start is crucial for maintaining a healthy relationship with your family. If you can't communicate openly about your mixed-race relationship from the beginning, it may cause long-term challenges in both your relationship and family dynamics.

Raising mixed kids

Raising kids is generally not easy, but raising mixed kids presents its own unique challenges. A moment at a birthday party when one of the girls asked, "Why isn't my hair growing like theirs? I want my hair longer." It was a large gathering of white people, with one Black couple and me. At that moment, everyone exchanged glances, and the mother turned to the girl and said, "Well, some hair types just don't grow as fast." Her voice was laced with uncertainty as she gauged the reactions around her. Everyone murmured, "Oh, shame," not out of malice but in sympathy for the mother having to explain such a complex issue.

There's an ongoing struggle to explain things in a way that doesn't offend anyone or damage a child's sense of self-worth. This is the reality many face. Educating your children can be tricky, especially when trying not to unintentionally reinforce racial or cultural biases. There's no manual for navigating either the relationship itself or the experience of raising mixed-race children, so education is key from the very start.

A friend and colleague of mine, who was married to a Zulu man, recently moved back to Durban to reconnect with her daughter's heritage and culture. They now live in a beautiful house surrounded by palm trees, with 3,000 square feet of space, a garden, a play area for her daughter, and a pool for fun. If you're familiar with South Africa, you can picture this home in a predominantly white suburb—quiet, peaceful, and filled with fresh, breezy air.

Here's her story: At the time, she was working from home and needed some quiet time to focus on an online meeting. She decided to send her daughter to the playground with her Zulu mother-in-law, hoping to get some work done. But while sitting in her office, she received a call from the nanny saying they couldn't let her daughter into the playground. The reason? The playground was filled with only white kids and their parents, and her daughter wasn't welcome to join in.

The next day at work, she came to me for advice. "Hey, I need your help," she said. I replied, "Hi Jess, how can I help?" She then shared the entire story and asked, "How do I explain this to my daughter? How do we have a conversation about race?" I responded, "Aren't they a little young?" My daughters were 9 and 6 at the time, and her daughter was just 5. My response was, "At what age is it okay to start that conversation?" I didn't think they were ready for a serious discussion on such a complex issue. My suggestion was to let them enjoy their childhood a bit longer before exposing them to such social challenges. It's important that they're ready to understand, and these lessons need to be communicated in a way they can grasp. Taking your time to participate in these discussions is key. You don't have to agree, but I believe they should be allowed to experience their childhood joy and innocence for as long as possible before the world complicates it.

Similar situations can also arise in schools, particularly if your mixed-race children are attending an all-white school, all-Indian, or all-black school. That's why it's always best to choose more multicultural than monocultural. But that's not always the reality when it comes to making choices. Ethier way, It's also crucial to be prepared for difficult conversations with teachers when incidents occur, handling them in a calm, informative manner. Focus on promoting a non-biased, non-racial approach from both sides. Prepare yourself—it may feel like a battlefield at times, but the effort will be worth it. By advocating for your children, you'll help raise strong, intelligent individuals and make a positive impact on the lives of others.

You are raising future leaders

You are raising future leaders — make no mistake about it. These children embody a remarkable blend of genetic potential. Their brains are wired for creativity and intelligence, especially since they've been exposed to at least three languages from birth. This linguistic richness sparks their creativity and sharpens their minds. They have incredible skills and absorb information like sponges, but they need our support to thrive.

It's essential to recognize their unique gifts and personalities. It's our responsibility to nurture and develop these talents. Through learning, training, and building over the years, we can help them master their strengths and become the individuals they are destined to be.

Those children will be the future peacemakers between nations. They possess a unique ability to understand both sides of any issue, embodying the best of both worlds and are more open-minded. Take a German-Ethiopian mix, for example — they are ideally positioned to bridge the cultural and social differences between these two countries in a harmonious way. Their grasp of multiple languages and communication styles, as well as an understanding of how systems function, is a remarkable asset. This can foster understanding, facilitate business deals, and even smooth political relationships. The same goes for all intercultural unity.

Here it is to convey this: amidst all the challenges and tough days you face, remember who you are raising. You've been entrusted with the responsibility to nurture these future leaders. When you feel emotionally drained by intercultural issues, cultural norms, or racial offenses, remind yourself that you hold a diamond in your hands. Sometimes, that diamond needs to be polished and even endure some heat to shine brilliantly and dispel darkness. Your role is to bring light to them. Not letting darkness, hate, and intolerance grow as close cultural relationships grow.

Unified Approaches to School Systems and Community Support Networks

How many international schools do you think exist in Africa alone? What about in Asia or around the world? When talking about international schools, it's not referring to those that simply label themselves as such. It refers to schools that are officially supported by their home countries, like Russian or German embassy schools. These schools are backed by their governments and follow the national curriculum of their respective countries.

Now, consider the students who attend these schools. Some are admitted because they can afford the high tuition, others for college applications, or because they hold the passport of that country. These children are not always full nationals of the country; they might be of mixed heritage, children of expatriates working for companies from that country, or even African children who hold foreign passports. For example, a child from an Ethiopian family might have a US passport. This creates complexity, as communication styles and values can vary depending on the family's background and how long they've lived abroad. The principles of these families can differ greatly from those who have never left their home country.

In such situations, teachers and educators need to approach their work with greater sensitivity and understanding, recognizing the diverse needs of these students. This challenge affects not just educators but also parents. To support children in the way they need — by listening to them, understanding them, and helping them succeed academically — there are many factors to consider, especially psychological needs and the principles that should be embraced. This topic is worth exploring further so we can simplify the process and make things easier for everyone involved.

What does it mean to attend an international or interracial school?

First, let's clarify what an international school is and, in this context, what an interracial school means. Over the past decade, the world has become more interconnected. People are traveling more and working abroad, and interracial marriages have become increasingly common.

This has led to a faster pace of cultural blending than ever before. We have started to see the world beyond the communities where we were raised, moving to new places and even deciding to make them our homes. As a result, many of us have become deeply integrated into cultures and races different from our own.

Now, children are growing up navigating multiple cultures, sometimes balancing two or even three different cultural identities. This can be confusing, especially during their formative years. Let's be honest—adults still experience confusion about where they belong. But when it comes to children, these questions and challenges are even more pronounced. They often struggle to process their experiences without guidance, which is why, as parents and educators, we are responsible for supporting their growth and development.

This is where international and interracial schools come in. These schools play a crucial role in providing a safe and supportive environment for students to navigate their identities. They should offer a system that fosters mental, physical, and emotional well-being. Being an international or interracial school means that these institutions are uniquely positioned to help students understand and integrate their diverse backgrounds.

Now that we've set the stage, let's explore how we can address these challenges. Don't misunderstand this—this is not as a preschool teacher, but as a parent and educator; the school environments can address issues that arise later in life by starting early. Many of the difficulties society faces in schools today could have been prevented by a little more confronting and addressing issues rather than avoiding dealing with them. Mental breakdowns, kids getting involved in bad behaviors, and psychological instability can be avoided if teachers pay attention. Listen to the kids to actually listen and not defend their ego or the reputation of schools.

What makes teaching mixed-heritage children unique?

Unlike previous generations, today's children are exposed to an overwhelming amount of information at an unprecedented pace. They are constantly bombarded with both scientific and non-scientific data, news, and people's opinions. They have access to real-time information about what is happening around the world, a far cry from how things were when we were growing up. Back in our day, information came through written letters or newspapers — carefully proofread and checked before being printed for public access, usually on specific days. The news we received about far-off places was limited, and unless something major happened, it was rare to know what was truly going on elsewhere in the world.

Today, traveling is easier than ever, thanks to the growth of the airline industry and greater access to wealth, which allows families to afford flights. Children now take holidays to visit family members or simply for fun, flying across continents. In contrast, when we were kids, if someone abroad wanted to update us, they would send a letter that took months to arrive. And even then, it often wouldn't tell the full truth, as they might not want to worry you. Today's kids, however, know everything. If they want to learn about global issues or events, they can easily search for answers online and access a wealth of information at their fingertips.

This raises an important question: how can we, as educators and caregivers, help these children navigate all this information and grow in the right direction? Are educational institutions taking the necessary steps to filter out misinformation while encouraging positive learning? How are we supporting their development into healthy, successful adults? Are we truly listening to them and understanding their needs? Change is inevitable, but how do we guide them in a way that prepares them for the challenges ahead?

Teaching today's children is not easy, especially when they are exposed to so much. However, it is essential that we focus on helping them become mentally and physically healthy, strong, and successful individuals. The question is: how can we do that effectively in this fast-paced, information-rich world?

How can we help children grow into the best version of themselves and use their differences to their advantage?

History has shown us that when society undergoes major changes, it often feels like a storm we can't control. This uncertainty scares us because we don't fully understand what these changes will bring or how to process them. It's unsettling not knowing how to guide our children or what the future holds for them. Most of us fear losing control and not knowing what tomorrow will look like. Yet, these "stormy" times often bring about remarkable progress. They lead to innovations, stronger leaders, and smarter solutions in business, healthcare, politics, and more.

This is why it's crucial to explore how you can help turn these changes into positive outcomes. How can you use these challenges, differences, and shifting backgrounds to benefit humanity? Rather than fuelling negativity, we need to channel our energy and resources in a way that aligns with a higher purpose, whether that's God's plan or the universe's design. Instead of resisting change, how can we nurture future leaders who are strong, resilient, and capable rather than raising a generation of complainers and weak-minded individuals?

As educators, you need a strong perspective on change. The adults cannot afford to be complainers themselves while expecting to lead and guide the children. All must step up and execute this huge responsibility effectively. It's time to set aside personal fears and focus on the duty we all have in this era. One must recognize the curiosity of young minds and give them the room to explore and ask questions. They are bombarded with information daily, far beyond what we are teaching them in school. To help them, we must truly listen to their concerns.

When a child comes to teachers for help, it is better to rejoice in their willingness to communicate rather than shutting them out. This is a sign that they trust you enough to share their worries. Each teacher must consider their age, developmental stage, capacity for absorbing information, and emotional maturity. Just because they appear older or sound more knowledgeable doesn't mean they're beyond their need for guidance. It is mandatory to avoid treating them like adults when their emotional and mental development is still unfolding.

As educators, it's essential to remain calm and not react impulsively. Everything we say and do in these moments can significantly impact the child's future well-being. The responses should be thoughtful and informed, based on both the child's input and our professional expertise. It's necessary to set aside personal biases or fears shaped by external opinions or casual conversations. Educators hold the future of these children in the hands of the teachers, and the time you spend with them is precious.

So, the approach you should take is simple: **Rejoice** – in their openness; **Recognize** – where they are in their development; **Remain** – calm and composed; **Respond** – thoughtfully, using the knowledge and tools we have to guide them toward a positive future.

Core Lesson

When families and communities support cross-cultural love, children thrive in strength and identity.

8

Crafting Your Path to Victory: The Journey of Healing and Self-Discovery

You Are Constantly Training for Victory

Don't be scared. A battle doesn't necessarily involve swords and guns like the movies you watch or the war books you've read. It can be a spiritual or emotional struggle that life puts us through to survive. In this context, we're focusing on those aspects. If it comes to physical confrontation, that's domestic violence, and it must be reported. I'm referring to the spiritual and emotional battles we face, as well as the mental and mindset training needed to navigate the challenges of daily life.

So, what is the battle we're talking about here?

The Fights

There are three different fights, and you don't necessarily face all three in one day. They vary in intensity and seasonality. In one season, you might confront one battle, while in another, it could be a different one. Sometimes, you may experience a mixture of two or even all three.

The Fight with Yourself

This fight involves constantly questioning whether the choices you're making are the right ones. It brings a wave of uncertainty and thoughts that are impossible to escape. Did I make the right decision? Can I really handle this? I need to change. I'll never learn this, and so on. It's a continuous struggle in your mind, manifesting as feelings or thoughts. Whether it's related to the past, present, or future you desperately want to get right, it requires training. Just like any battle, this one demands that we constantly train our thoughts and focus on winning so we can conquer our circumstances and cultivate a willingness to be happy and stable.

Coming back to our topic, you know that you love this person, but you're unsure if you can fully trust them to embark on this journey and take all these risks together. Can I genuinely say that this is MY PERSON? Someone I can rely on when I need support or if I become ill? Your mind will constantly grapple with these mixed feelings of doubt and trust. As a result, you might find yourself stuck in a cycle of being half in, half out of the relationship, especially during disagreements that feel disproportionately weighted — like a 75:25 split. It's during these times that the struggle becomes even more pronounced. Ultimately, it's up to you to decide whether to step in and fight for it.

This book is designed to help you prepare and train yourself so that you can succeed in this battle of uncertainty. And it starts with you. Everything you've heard, known, and experienced up to this point has shaped your thinking at this moment. Every decision you've made has been influenced by the knowledge you've acquired since birth. Some of this knowledge is essential for survival, like the instinct not to touch fire, which you either learned from someone else or through firsthand experience of its consequences. These lessons can be good or bad, beautiful or traumatic, but they all teach us valuable things, whether for better or worse.

If you want to make this work, you need to adjust your approach to your personal battles. To do that, you must pivot your focus. Our minds tend to cling to negative thoughts rather than letting them go, so it's essential to train your mind to focus on the positive.

For example, if you love a healthy lifestyle and want to give up unhealthy eating, you might say, "I won't eat chocolate anymore." Now, it's up to you to train your mind to think of a comforting, healthy soup instead of chocolate all the time. You must consciously choose to make the right decisions today for your well-being.

Similarly, you need to choose to focus on the good and the love in your relationship instead of dwelling on negative thoughts. To win this struggle, stop fixating on the worst experiences and avoid constantly meditating on them. Replace those unhealthy thoughts with something that nurtures your growth, both personally and in your relationship.

The Fight with Your Partner

Until our first daughter was five years old, my partner and I constantly argued about finances. I was so traumatized that I wanted to leave him, so I packed my things and moved into a new apartment. Yet, there was something I always remembered whenever I considered giving up during those five years: my mom's advice. She said, "The first three to five years of marriage are the hardest. After that, you learn so much more about each other that it becomes easier, nicer, and more intimate year by year. You will truly have a partner for life—someone you love and who loves you, someone who has your back in tough times. So hang in there. It gets easier." She was right about that.

However, the battles with our partner don't stop there. You simply gain a better understanding of each other's needs, wants, love languages, and all those little nuances. Remember that while it gets easier, forms of conflict will still arise. What helps during these battles is the ability to see beyond the conflict. Consider what the "enemy" is trying to achieve: to break you as a person, to fracture your partnership, or to disrupt the peace and love in your home.

Even worse, some battles aim to tear the family apart. Others test whether your unity can withstand the storm. If you can see past the immediate struggle and recognize what the enemy is after, you'll know when to surrender, have important conversations, and, most importantly, avoid saying or doing something that could hand your home over to the enemy. You must choose to save your God-given partner and emerge victorious.

The War in Relationships with Others

This fight can be more challenging as you are with this person every day. You are both emotionally, socially, financially, and culturally invested in each other by now. You face many things on a daily basis. Simply going out and meeting people can trigger certain things. Colleagues and family members often see your partner as a goddess. Without exaggerating, especially if that partner is white or comes from one of the economically stable or wealthier countries. While the other is praised, one of the underdeveloped or poorest countries will be mistreated or stared at. Sometimes, one is seen as a charity case and the other as a donor. Until they get to know the person well, many will view one of you as someone lucky enough to have won the lottery to a better life rather than as a couple trying to build a life together.

Eventually, that "charity case" mentality creeps in. You start to let people assume what they want. You grow tired of convincing others that you are more than just a pretty face and that you have something valuable to offer the world. So, you meet people and listen to their assumptions as they talk about themselves. You don't want to show them that you're doing well—financially, emotionally, or romantically. These seemingly small things can profoundly affect your relationships over time. You start to doubt people. You question their kindness: Why is he so nice? Why does she come all the way here to visit me? You begin to pull away from others unless they have some kind of international experience, preferably in mixed relationships. Otherwise, communication becomes difficult due to fears of judgment.

When you first met your partner, he was perhaps 30 and had just moved to Mozambique with a debt of 6,000 euros. You recently returned from your study abroad, and you are on your way to a career on a good path, having completed your BSc. You join an international organization and run a successful project while waiting for your further study abroad to be finalized. Then you met this guy from France, and things got serious. You move in together and decide to give up your further studies because you don't want to leave him. You tell yourself you could pursue that later. So, you stay and continue with ICT projects, leaving your masters behind completely. Now, ten years later, you look back and wonder what might have happened if you had made a different decision. Do you believe your life would have been easier if you had followed your initial plan to leave your country again? Would it have been different if you had married someone from your own culture? You will never know. But one thing you can be sure of is that this relationship and the sacrifices you make were not and will not be easy.

So, how do you move forward? How do you win this ongoing struggle to find normal relationships around you without questioning motives? How do you overcome this endless battle of forming lasting connections? Here are a few things we need to understand:

The Responsibility

The sooner you understand the responsibilities that come with it, the faster you can start living and enjoying your life. One of the key responsibilities is to avoid making decisions based on fear. Instead, focus on making well-thought-out choices. Accept that your life is not perfect. Trust your instincts regarding the decisions you've made, and learn to take responsibility for them.

The Victory and the Healing Process

Nothing brings a warrior greater joy than both victory and the lessons learned along the way. After enduring all the battles, if you're strong enough to withstand the struggles and not let them break you, victory will be yours. You've come to understand yourself and those around you in this new chapter of life, and the feeling is freeing. You're lighter, happier, and now fully equipped to handle whatever comes your way. You've learned how to communicate smoothly and navigate any situation with ease. You can now enjoy productive, meaningful moments with loved ones or colleagues from diverse backgrounds.

Your unity—whether with people of different races or countries—is making a profound impact. The children born from these connections play significant roles in shaping the world, contributing to both social and economic growth. Your Turkish and Ethiopian partnership, for example, is fostering job creation and community development in Africa. Business deals are flourishing with Turkish investors in the production and export industries. Through initiatives like Tenachin and Buket of Hope, healthcare transformation is underway, improving nutrition and preventative care at the grassroots level.

Your European and African collaborations through Iceaddis are driving technological advancements, the very first tech startup and coworking space in the country, enhancing education and financial support and enabling young people to launch their own businesses that address Ethiopia's socio-economic challenges. The work of Menchen Für Menchen, building schools and investing in capacity-building projects, is creating lasting generational change. Despite the hurdles, you've remained committed to helping communities and creating a positive impact—

raising funds even when others didn't believe in your mission.

When you look back on these success stories, you'll see that every victory was preceded by struggle. But in overcoming those obstacles, you've contributed to making the world a better place. Now, you're proud you never gave up and kept pushing forward. Your resilience has made all the difference.

Celebrating victory also involves a healing process that requires time and patience. Healing begins with acknowledging the wound and treating it. Whatever caused the pain must have already been addressed in order for true healing to occur. Once you've faced it, avoid revisiting it or dwelling on it. If necessary, seek professional support. Surround yourself with a supportive community that encourages healing. Don't interrupt the process by repeatedly picking at the wound. Engage in activities that nurture your recovery, much like how doctors recommend light walking after surgery to promote healing. Once healed, let go of the injuries and move beyond the victim mentality. Celebrate the victory, as the battles were not in vain. Only once the struggles have passed will you see their purpose. These experiences taught you valuable lessons and built an inner strength you never knew you had. Release the hurt, let go of grudges, and stop focusing on past betrayals or complaints. Move forward and embrace the life ahead of you.

Let Go of the Victim Mentality and the Ego!

Life doesn't owe you anything. It's time to shed the entitlement mindset that expects you to be treated like royalty. You must take the initiative and earn the respect you seek. Merely saying, "I deserve to be respected," or "I deserve this and that," won't get you anywhere. You have to actively pursue what you want.

Engage with others, but establish clear boundaries. Approach requests with respect and politely decline when necessary. Remember, it's perfectly fine if some people don't like you — some will admire you, while others may not. Accepting this is essential.

A friend from India once asked, "Do you know why we succeed when entering the world?" When I asked why, he responded, "You can't offend us. Insults or saying 'go away' won't deter us." He pointed out that an Indian will persist in selling whatever needs to be sold, undeterred by rejection. That's what works.

Similarly, in the challenges we've discussed, playing the victim won't help you. If you aim to continue to succeed, you need to keep a winning attitude. Along the way, release your ego. True success comes from actively pursuing what you desire. To do that, you'll need to navigate through challenges and setbacks as they come. The fights you have had so far now have taught you how to fight. As new challenges arise, you rise to the occasion, learn from your mistakes, adapt your strategies, and keep moving forward to overcome the obstacles in all your relationships.

Many people start to feel uncomfortable when they don't see anyone who looks like them in their neighborhood or in a crowd they're part of. Walking into a restaurant where no one resembles you can be intimidating for some. But try to look at it this way: the Earth is everyone's playground. Why should you be excluded from any part of it? Everyone else around you is just another person enjoying the same space. So let go of the fear and stop seeing yourself as a victim. Embrace the experience, and start enjoying life to its fullest.

There Is No "We" Until You Learn to Win Together

When you experience success in life, it's easy to fall into the mindset of "I did this," "I accomplished that," focusing on your individual efforts. However, emphasizing individuality too much can lead to problems. As a couple, it's essential to shift from "I" to "we." This person has stood by you through both the good and bad times, and when success comes, it should feel like a shared victory.

In the early days of dating or the first few years of marriage, it's natural to think in terms of "I" and "you," each maintaining a separate sense of self. But as time goes on, especially after those initial years, it's crucial to embrace a united mindset. While you may have lived independently before, making choices on your own, once you're together, it's important to think and act as a team at every stage of your life. This unity should be present not only during struggles but also in moments of triumph.

You always have parts of "I," "you," and "we." Often, it's easy to concentrate on individual careers, personal happiness, and self-interests, neglecting the shared accomplishments and joy in your partnership. Over time, this focus can create distance between you and your partner. As you drift apart, it becomes easier for life's challenges to threaten your connection. Any strain on your relationship can jeopardize your unity. Begin as individuals, but work towards building unity. Face challenges together, celebrate victories as one, and continue to enjoy life side by side.

It's crucial to make time for each other and nurture the "we." Even with children, prioritize date nights and getaways to strengthen your connection. Feed your relationship with what it needs before it starts to fade.

The Power of Crafting & Building Your Own Path

After everything you've chosen and accomplished, there are times when you look back and find yourself blaming certain things for what has happened to you. You might think that what's happening to you is a result of your actions, or perhaps you attribute it to the government, your partner, society, family members who have done or failed to do something, or even some natural force punishing you for something. At times, you're also from blaming your parents or siblings.

No, you shouldn't. And here's why: As discussed earlier, letting go is crucial. When you're in the process of building a new path, there may be times when you feel tempted to look back and get lost in those past moments, especially when it feels difficult to build alone. Sometimes, as you create a new life with a partner no one approves of, it can be isolating. In some cases, people may accept your relationship, but they won't offer the support you need to build it, leaving you to build on your own. For others, while they approve of your union, they can't offer help because you're living in a different country, and you're left to navigate challenges alone. During these frustrating times, the urge to blame can resurface. However, giving in to this temptation will only hinder your healing, as it's like reopening a wound that's been healing — making it harder to move forward. Blaming others in these moments blocks your energy and your ability to continue building the new life you're striving for.

The decision to blame only yourself is one that you must make for your own well-being. When you make choices based on what you truly want out of life, you take full responsibility for the outcomes and recognize that you are in control. This mindset also helps nurture loving and meaningful relationships, as it enables you to create an environment of mutual respect and understanding. Life is your journey — your house, your vision, your path to where you want to reach. Why let others interfere with that? Design your life the way you want it. Put in the effort, make the sacrifices, and remember that life is full of changes. Policies, people, and situations will evolve, and those things are often beyond your control.

Things can change quickly. You may have everything planned — finances in order, an acceptance letter for your dream school, and the excitement of moving abroad — only to find yourself blocked from entering the country. Or perhaps you feel financially secure with a solid bank balance, only to watch the value decrease dramatically over a few months. Markets fluctuate, natural disasters strike, and pandemics occur, all outside your control. What matters is how you respond: your choices, perspective, the people you let into your life, where you choose to live, the studies or job paths you take, and how you treat others. These decisions are yours to make. And when you're in a relationship, especially with someone from a different background or income level, these decisions can become even more challenging. The key is to act when the right opportunities come your way — don't delay. This brings us to the next important topic.

Take the power of Your New House – be the architect who creates a unique design.

Every new method or invention arises from our evolving human needs. Similarly, interracial couples, cross-country relationships, and mixed-race children need to understand the immense beauty and power they hold. Not only do they bring unity and help break down divisions, but they also have the potential to make significant economic, political, and social impacts. For all of this to succeed, it is essential that they maintain peace of mind, stay focused, and nurture happiness at home.

Today, it's undeniable that the world is more interconnected than ever — not just through technology but through personal relationships. As the world becomes more intertwined, building an interracial home has become easier than in the past. People are leaving their hometowns to start new lives elsewhere due to migration or to address the world crisis, and many are forming relationships with partners from around the globe. Interracial couples are now more common, with unions between people from countries like Japan and Ethiopia, Germany and South Africa, Japan and the U.S., France and Eritrea, and many more. It's truly remarkable to witness how far society has come.

From a time when mixed-race relationships were criminalized to an era where they were merely tolerated but not fully accepted, we've made significant progress. While interracial unions are now more widely tolerated, challenges remain in normalizing marriages and partnerships between people from different countries. Though we've made great strides, the path forward still requires continued effort. While many studies have been conducted, few focus on providing guidance for interracial couples as they navigate life together. Finding ways to build a happy, thriving home and tackle the challenges they face in both social and personal relationships is essential. Understanding and embracing this journey empowers couples, giving them the strength to continue building their lives together.

Now that you've moved past blaming others and embraced the power of building, it's time to understand what true power is and how to use it effectively. When you establish your own space or claim your territory, no one can easily come in and disturb your peace. This sense of ownership keeps you grounded, preventing distractions and manipulation. With a clear mind, you're able to stay focused and take the necessary steps to nurture the new unity and family you've created while also supporting your extended family.

Now, you are deeply connected to your goals in life, and your bond with your partner has grown stronger as you plan together. Having established your boundaries, cleared your hearts, and created a united home, no one's opinions or suggestions can easily distract you. This newfound sense of control empowers both of you to shape your happiness together. You now know exactly what to do for your partner and how to help them grow alongside you. Your relationship becomes more resilient. Once your home is strong and stable, you can connect with others without fear of fragility.

Opening your doors to new possibilities becomes easier as the foundation you've built is solid. Without these strengths and insights, your dream home might never reach completion — or worse, it could collapse entirely. The power of your new home now has the potential to make a meaningful impact on the world. Your home is a crucial part of the larger picture, a stepping stone towards the broader change and impact that the world is waiting for.

Many types of relationships and living arrangements that are common today didn't exist in the past. Often, there are no established policies to accommodate the specific paperwork needed for your living situation, financial access, insurance, or even the paperwork required by embassies and countries. This is especially true for families like yours, where you're among the first to make such requests. If these systems don't yet exist, it's up to you to help create them. You have the power to build a new home and design the life you want, crafting everything necessary for the household you've established.

This unity and strength are paving the way for future generations, ensuring they don't face the same challenges you've encountered. Over time, you'll begin to see the fruits of your efforts as the paths you've created start to make it easier for others to follow in your footsteps.

The Power of Adjustments

Things don't always go as planned. Your life might not have unfolded the way you envisioned. The uncontrollable things might happen. You may have thought you'd stay in one country for just a few years, change jobs by now, or that raising kids would be easier. You might have imagined you'd be married or have built your own home by now. Everyone has different expectations, but unfortunately, life sometimes doesn't always align with those hopes. Sacrifices and compromises are often necessary along the way. Learn to pivot.

The previous chapters have emphasized the importance of being mindful of the implications of your decisions. Are you truly comfortable with what they entail? You've come a long way, and in life, anything can happen. When changes arise, make sure to have an open conversation with your partner, thoroughly discussing what these changes mean for both of you. Don't make decisions based purely on the excitement of new beginnings without fully understanding their consequences.

Then comes the need for adjustment. In life and relationships, you'll need to master the art of pivoting when things don't go as planned. Sometimes, certain paths simply aren't meant for you. The universe may guide you toward what truly aligns with you, or it may have a completely different plan. Remember, some situations and people are temporary. So, don't dwell on the departure of certain people from your life. There will be times of financial success, and there will also be moments of hard work and persistence. Adjust your expectations, your work discipline, and your focus accordingly. You can't have strawberries year-round; you harvest what you can and preserve it for later.

When seasons and circumstances don't align, think about how you can adapt to sustain yourself through the winters of life. Learn to adapt as needed. Focus on what you can accomplish with the time, environment, and resources available to you in the present moment. Avoid getting stuck in thoughts of "I could have" or "I should have" if you had made different choices. Instead, learn from your experiences, appreciate what you have, and make the most of it.

Acknowledge and Embrace the Challenges of Walking This Path

As I mentioned at the beginning of this book, challenges are inevitable — from your dating days, through marriage and living together, all the way to having children. The goal remains unchanged: not to scare you, but to inform you. What you do with this information is entirely up to you. How you apply it to make things work in your unique situation depends on your circumstances and preferences. Ultimately, making informed decisions is far more valuable than stumbling through life and wasting time. You've come a long way to reach this point. Now that you've identified, evaluated, and gained a clear understanding of the challenges, it's time to acknowledge and embrace them — if you choose to continue down this cross-cultural path of life.

At times, this journey can feel incredibly lonely. You might find yourself surrounded by people yet still experience a deep sense of disconnect. Conversations can become unbearable, and you may catch yourself thinking, "Why am I listening to this nonsense? It's so mindlessly boring." They don't seem to care about what matters to you, talking about topics that are completely irrelevant to your values and beliefs. You might want to walk away, but it feels rude, so you remain, enduring what you don't enjoy.

The constant pressure from both sides of the family and community during holiday gatherings is another challenge. People asking, "So, are you teaching your kids German or Amharic now?" or saying, "They should speak their mother tongue." Even strangers seem to have opinions on whether your children speak the local language or not, adding to your frustration as you feel torn between two cultures, norms, and values.

You might struggle with wanting to protect your kids from confusion while also navigating their heritage and trying to understand where they truly belong. There are many more scenarios and challenges that could be mentioned, but they all stem from the same root and lead to the same conclusion.

Knowing these challenges is not enough. Acknowledging them, embracing them, and using them for growth is the best way forward. The key is to stop attaching too much importance to specific locations, traditions, and norms. Instead, detach from those constraints and attach yourselves to a new normal—the home you have built together.

Understand the Rewarding Outcome of Taking This Path

To succeed at anything, you must invest time, effort, and resources. Similarly, the path you're choosing—or about to choose—will lead you to situations that are emotionally, financially, and physically demanding. During these challenges, it's crucial to keep sight of the bigger picture. All those adversities do and did bring strength, connections, and creative ideas to solve the problems that needed to be solved.

When Karlheinz Böhm first flew to Ethiopia, leaving the acting career and magazine career and gathered donations with a strong heart and desire to help people. To address the unimaginable challenge in Ethiopia then, he used his opportunity of being a public show to get donations of 1.2 francs in 1981.

With the confidence of a newcomer, Böhm asked the authorities for land to move the starving semi-nomads from Babile to the fertile Erer Valley. Surprisingly, his request was approved, allowing 2,100 people to start fresh as independent farmers with help from Ethiopian staff Böhm hired. The settlers named their new village "Nagaya," meaning "peace," and Böhm kept his donors updated through reports, leading to the creation of Nagaya magazine. At first, experts mocked the project because Böhm lacked formal development training, but by 1983, the families were seeing successful harvests. But all the challenges didn't stop Böhm. He was listening to hear.

He knew what he wanted to do. He saw the bigger picture in all the potential challenges he would be facing.

Böhm's impact in Ethiopia is immense. His work has transformed countless lives, saving many through his dedication. He's built over a thousand projects, including schools, health centers, vocational training centers, and agricultural and construction projects throughout the country. But beyond the work, if you sit down with his last wife, Almaz Böhm — also Ethiopian — and his two children and ask, "How was this journey?" they would undoubtedly share the thousands of challenges they faced as a family. Perhaps the better question would be, "What kept you going?" Because without a clear vision of the bigger picture, such a path would have been nearly impossible to endure.

There are countless success stories that offer valuable lessons. Many individuals have made significant contributions to the socio-economic development of their home countries, fostered sustainable relationships between nations, and driven innovations in technology and business. These cross-country collaborations have paved the way for a better world. To name a few, Mulu (Ethiopian), Klaus (German), and comedian Tedros Teclebrahn all encountered their own unique struggles on their respective paths. Some persevered, while others gave up. Yet, those who strategized and adapted found ways to turn challenges into opportunities, achieving greater outcomes along the way.

Many colleagues abandoned their projects in South Africa when the challenges became too overwhelming. Some struggled with the constant frustration, where both business and non-business conversations turned traumatic. At times, the situation escalated to the point of being shot at for exposing corruption. People left. To endure such challenges, staying focused on the bigger picture becomes your anchor, helping you remain steady and keep moving forward. And some say this intercultural work or relationship is not for everyone. That's true. It takes immense self-discipline, courage, and the ability to control your willpower, all while showing kindness to others, no matter their background or how the world perceives them.

When relationships and family are involved, things can become even more complex. However, looking at Karl's son and daughter today, the role they're playing in transforming lives is nothing short of remarkable. Their intercultural connection has made one of the most significant contributions to society. Through creating jobs, driving economic change, and fostering deep social engagement, they've helped raise children who feel a sense of belonging in both the German and Ethiopian communities. This unity has brought together shared resources, all working toward a brighter future.

One of the most significant outcomes is the constant learning through the confusion of belonging, the challenges of solving problems independently, and the growth that comes with it. You, your children, and everyone around you have gained valuable knowledge, experienced rewarding personal growth, and, most importantly, developed resilience. You've acquired a rich understanding of the world, a broader view of humanity, empathy for others, and the ability to adapt wherever you go. This journey fosters tolerance for differences and the ability to bring unity in environments where others may focus on division.

Practice Visualising on the Bigger Picture: The Lasting Impact of This Choice

Establishing Tenachin (meaning "our health" in Ethiopia) Company was driven by a deep passion for helping people maintain their health and prevent health issues before they arise. When we first moved to South Africa, we were unsure of where to begin, how to connect with people, or how to execute such a project. Initially, we didn't know anyone, and as is often the case, it took two years of learning and understanding the local landscape to build a community and form connections with wellness centers.

At the same time, the project also aimed to gather donations to support low-income communities in Ethiopia, providing them with basic food and clothing on a yearly basis. Over time, we began hosting events to educate the community on how they can take proactive steps to prevent health problems before they occur. As healthcare costs continue to rise, prevention has proven to be the most effective way to manage both the capacity and demand for medical care.

Throughout the nine years Tenachin has existed, the challenges have been unimaginable. However, what kept us moving forward was our deep involvement in the community. We united South African, Ethiopian, American, and German forces to contribute to society. We hosted wellness events in Durban, ran a GoFundMe page for the Bucket of Hope Project with the help of people in the U.S., and supported local startups and initiatives focused on job creation. We also received funding from Germany for projects that foster job creation through the efforts of young entrepreneurs, returning experts, and diasporas who share the same vision of bringing resources together to create a lasting impact.

These are the things that will keep you going, the things that will truly nourish your soul. Often overlooked, but the true joy and fulfillment in life come when part of your heart is dedicated to helping others. Whether it's brightening someone's day, making them smile, or helping them fulfill their wishes, this act of kindness will bring you closer to your purpose. Deep down, you know you have a reason for being here, and it's important to recognize that you play a role in making a meaningful impact in the world.

Seeing the world as a whole and practicing the art of visualization is essential to achieving your goals. When challenges come, things don't go as planned, conflicts arise, or others try to silence you for exposing wrongdoings, it's crucial to remind yourself why you are on this path. Ask yourself, "Could this relationship be bigger than this? What greater purpose might it serve?" Believe it or not, it does have a purpose—purpose for you, your family, your community, your country, and the world at large.

Every experience, both good and bad, has its purpose. So, each day, take time to reflect. Go within and reconnect with your purpose. Reimagine the bigger picture and choose to live each day with that purpose in mind. Walk forward with patience, love, and kindness toward humanity as you take your next steps.

Core Lesson

Healing begins when you release the victim mindset and build a life of victory together.

9

Final Touch to Breaking Stereotypes and Reinventing Yourself

The Perception About That Country: Why It Matters

You are wrong about the country. Yes, you are! But don't take offense—hear this out. You may think you know a lot about your own country, but the truth is, it's always a learning process. Very few people know everything about their country, let alone about others. Most are familiar with only the highlights of it all. The beauty of life lies in recognizing what you know, accepting that you don't know certain things, and choosing to keep learning. Instead of assuming, ask questions—what and why?

In this world, we often form opinions about places based on what the media tells us or what others say. Let's avoid falling into stereotypes. Most importantly, let's stop generalizing people based on their country of origin—it's the wrong approach. You'll always be wrong at some point, and you'll end up disappointing yourself and others. So, why go down that path? Instead, ask yourself: If you thought like a foreigner, could you truly appreciate the beauty of any city in Africa? When people talk about South Africa, they often mention crime. When Ethiopia comes up, it's about tribal conflicts and hunger. The U.S. is often linked to its history of slavery and ongoing gun violence. And when people think of Germany, they remember Hitler and the Holocaust.

Sadly, the issues people associate with certain countries tend to overshadow the beauty that truly lies within. Outsiders often focus on the negatives, making it hard to see the rich landscapes, delicious food, or the warmth of the culture. It becomes exhausting to constantly explain the positive aspects of your home when the world chooses to focus on the worst. Deep down, you know there's so much more to your country than you see. So do that.

The same applies to how people view one another. They see you and immediately form conclusions without taking the time to truly get to know you. We rarely ask ourselves if maybe we should talk to them first. Without communication, there can be no understanding. Imagine seeing someone in a bar—you can't expect to marry them just based on their looks. The same goes for making assumptions about countries or people from specific places.

Now ask yourself: where are you from, and what stereotypes does your country face? That's exactly how others perceive you when they first meet you. So, how does that make you feel? Probably not great, right? Now consider: have you ever judged someone just because they're from a particular country? Have you made assumptions without truly getting to know them?

Why, then, do we allow ourselves to do something we despise when it's done to us? How does that make you feel? If we all took a moment to evaluate our actions and judgments based on simple principles, perhaps we could start making a real difference in this world. "Do unto others as you would have them do unto you." For every action in life, there's a reaction. You harvest what you sow. You know all these, right? Now, sow a good seed and watch it grow. No matter what you believe, remember that your actions have consequences.

When you first meet your husband or wife, you may not have a deep understanding of European history, aside from the obvious, especially the impact of World War II on the European people and, most importantly, the German people. You approach the relationship with excitement, imagining the romantic journey you've always envisioned. It's beautiful, but there are so many things you don't quite understand about him and his family — how he feels about certain things, how people treat them in different places, or how some still carry the weight of a broken heart from the past. At times, he may worry about your family attending a Christmas market together for safety reasons. Your own naïve ignorance allows you to enjoy moments without being weighed down by fear or concerns for your surroundings. This happened similarly when he was in certain places in some of the African countries you traveled to or lived in.

Your partner is an incredible person, and together, you share an amazing and adventurous journey. As Einstein once said, "One must be intentionally ignorant to succeed in this world." Your lack of knowledge about Europe's troubled past allowed you to see him for who he truly is, untouched by biases or the opinions of others — who often speak without truly understanding the situation.

As time goes on, you'll inevitably meet more people who ask questions shaped by the history of Hitler or the negative experiences others have had living in Germany. Over time, you may start noticing biased comments directed at both you and your partner — some of them even quite harsh. For instance, you might hear someone say, "Oh, Ethiopian girls love their phones," when, in reality, it's your partner who is always on his phone, scrolling through Spiege.de.

The main takeaway here is simple: Don't make assumptions. Stay open-minded and be willing to see things from a different perspective. Be willing to learn by experiencing the country, the people, and the person himself/herself. Stop following the crowd and viewing the world through other people's eyes. Whether you meet someone on a plane, at work, or even during your morning run, choose to be intentionally non-judgmental.

When it comes to relationships, it's crucial that you see your partner for who they truly are. Be open to learning about their country's history, culture, and upbringing. When you get serious with someone or marry someone from a different country, make the decision to understand them on your own terms. Not in someone else's eyes or understanding. Experience each other fully, enjoy the journey together, and learn from one another. Don't turn your relationship into an experiment to validate or challenge the stereotypes others have about their country. Turn your relationship into a mutual growth journey.

Kill Old Version of You! Yes, That You!

The new version of you, along with fresh life and relationships, often requires letting go of the past—much like starting a new business. Success doesn't come if you're only partially committed, right? The same rule applies to your marriage: if you're not fully invested in making it work, there's a high chance it won't succeed. So, ask yourself, "Are you willing to do whatever it takes to make your marriage thrive and keep your family united?" If your answer is yes, then go all in. If not, don't waste your time, and certainly don't bring children into a relationship you're uncertain about from the start. It's not fair to anyone, and it's not worth it.

Don't get this wrong — you may find yourself making the mistake of walking the line for too long, listening to friends and family talk about the negative aspects of Germans. Over time, you might start seeing and learning about German history through their lens. The media often presents certain narratives through news stories and jokes, which can shape your perceptions. But then, when you visit Germany and meet people, it might be an entirely different experience. That's why, when you embark on a new relationship or a new path, you need to have an open and unbiased perspective. Don't let your views be influenced by the media, others' assumptions, or your own preconceived notions. Let go of your old ways. Your past experiences have shaped you and provided valuable lessons, but it's time to move forward. You can't reach new destinations in life if you're still carrying around old baggage.

The experiences shared here are meant to help you understand the facts, learn from the mistakes and achievements of others, and ultimately live a more informed and fulfilling life with fewer disappointments. By doing so, you can build better relationships and develop a broader perspective on the socio-dynamics of the world, particularly in cross-cultural relationships. Understand that people will always have opinions or make comments about things they know nothing about. In the past, you might have reacted defensively, but in this new version of yourself, you educate and move forward with grace.

One last example: After 15 years of marriage, you arrive at the airport in your original home country, where you unexpectedly run into a high school classmate after 21 years. You introduce him to your husband and kids, and he remarks, "You had so many people after you, and you married a German?!" Kind of with a disappointed face. He is also married and has kids. But you choose not to say anything about his wife in response. Should you have? No! It is always wrong if you go low when people go low. It is also bad to be offended right away and say something that has no purpose other than making the other person feel bad.

Here's how the new you handle it: If this had happened 10 or even 12 years ago, it might have broken you or made you question the wonderful choice you made for yourself and your beautiful family. You might have responded defensively, feeling deeply disrespected and hurt. But over the years, you've realized that sometimes people speak or make assumptions out of ignorance. Often, some people just say nonsense to bring you down or to feel better about themselves by insulting you.

Now, you truly know what you need and who you are. You believe in what you're doing. Whether through experience or reading this book, you and your partner have learned how to handle situations like this. You've become anchored, standing by your partner and kids no matter what. Now, you've developed that thick skin everyone talks about when they speak of resilience and strength. After all that growth, nothing can hurt you deeper than what you allow.

The key takeaway here is this: to be truly happy and make informed decisions without bias, stay grounded in your own mindset. Don't let anyone pull you in different directions when it comes to choices that affect your life. If you didn't know something before, that's completely fine. Everyone starts somewhere. The first step is acknowledging what you don't know. Once you realize that, it's time to educate yourself—read, learn, and surround yourself with people who can help you grow. If you've heard negative stories or judgments, let go of those perceptions and do your own research. Choose to start fresh and experience things for yourself firsthand.

Simply put, it is like this. Have you ever had a friend rave about a restaurant's chicken curry, only to find it so awful that you felt like you were going to vomit? You once tried Bunny Chow after hearing great reviews, and you couldn't swallow even one bite; you wanted to gag. You decided to never try Bunny Chow again because of that experience. Now you know that you don't like bunny chaw because you experienced it yourself. Experiencing it and knowing it yourself is a different story than what people tell you through their eyes, experiences, and through their taste buds.

Choose to approach life from your point of view. Live without expectations and experience it without the weight of others' misinformed opinions. Go in with the pure intention of enjoying the meal. And honey—happy eating! If it tastes bad, spit it out on your own terms. If it's delicious, keep savoring it. Your life is about to get so much yummier!

Core Lesson

Breaking stereotypes starts with letting go of the old you and daring to reinvent your story.

10

The Path Forward: Keeping Life Easy and Enjoyable

Recognizing the Toughest Challenges and How to Overcome Them

Each Other's Beliefs

By now, you've explored various communication skills and methods for constructive dialogue, both with yourself and with others around you. To simplify and highlight the key challenges you may face as you navigate life's beautiful yet often challenging experiences, consider using the SPESTU approach. This stands for Spiritual, Political, Economic, Social, Technological, and Universal understanding — six critical aspects of both yourself and the world around you.

These factors are often overlooked, but when you take a practical, hands-on approach to understanding them, they can make your life much easier. With the SPESTU framework in mind, it's time to dive into the details of recognizing and managing *personal differences, workplace diversity, religious beliefs, financial challenges,* and *social conflicts.*

Personal Differences

One evening, you're having a family dinner with your in-laws when your partner's mother says something that bothers you. The comment feels insulting—not only to your culture but also to a family member who is dining with you. Out of respect for elders, as is customary in your culture, you choose not to respond or ask for clarification about what she meant. However, in your partner's culture, it's important to address misunderstandings or offenses as soon as they arise. Their family values open communication, where self-expression and independence are encouraged, no matter one's age.

The evening continues with unspoken tension. Some of your family members are visibly displeased by the conversation at the table, but the issue remains unresolved. Once you get home, you try to make sense of what happened. Your partner finds it hard to understand why you didn't address the comment right away, thinking it's ridiculous to let it go. You explain that, in your culture, it's important not to disrespect elders, especially your mother-in-law. The conversation continues, but neither of you feels heard, leaving you with a sense of misunderstanding. This misunderstanding may lead to small feelings of resentment, which, if left unaddressed, can grow into something much bigger. Over time, this could create a rift between you and your partner as each of you defends your family's values. This tension could eventually spread to your relationship with your in-laws, creating distance and difficulty in resolving the situation.

When two people share the same cultural background, communication often comes naturally—almost as easy as breathing. However, in mixed-couple relationships, every conversation requires more thought and intentionality. Your family and personal identity play a vital role in shaping your relationships. Language barriers, communication styles, values, societal influences, and deeply ingrained family ethics all come into play and can significantly impact how you interact with each other. Identifying those and knowing them is the main step.

Once you've recognized the personal differences between you and your partner, the next step is to approach them in a healthier way. Start with open, honest communication about those differences. Pretending nothing is wrong, smiling when you're hurt, or making your partner think you enjoy something you don't will only lead to more conflict later. Be transparent—put everything on the table. Discuss where you can compromise and identify the areas that are difficult for you to accept or let go of.

Next, set clear boundaries. It's important to understand your partner's boundaries, but equally crucial to establish your own from the start. Address misunderstandings as they arise, but do so calmly and constructively. Be mindful of your words—consider whether what you're saying could be offensive, undermining, or disrespectful. Avoid name-calling or making stereotypical assumptions, both in your relationship and when discussing issues with your family.

Always take cultural sensitivities into account when talking about traditions, social norms, family histories, and behaviors—especially regarding tone, gestures, and body language. Like any relationship, learning to compromise is essential when necessary. Let go of the small things that disrupt your harmony but aren't significant in the bigger picture. Be flexible and open-minded about new practices and ways of doing things. Respect each other's interests, dreams, and careers. Understand that you are both distinct individuals with unique backgrounds, desires, and choices. Neither is more important than the other, and recognizing this helps maintain balance in your relationship. Acknowledge, through both actions and words, that you each have an equal need to be heard, loved, and respected.

If needed, seek professional support. If couples therapy isn't an option, consider connecting with other intercultural couples. Spending time with others in mixed relationships not only gives you a sense of belonging but also a group of people who hear and understand your challenges. They mostly face similar challenges, just in different aspects and they can offer valuable insights. It provides a sense of solidarity and a safe space to share experiences. These interactions can give you new perspectives and practical approaches, empowering you with strength and wisdom as you work to find a middle ground, maintaining love and harmony in your relationship.

Spend some time alone, reevaluate your actions, and seek guidance from within before running to others for advice. Again, don't run to people, especially to those who have not lived such a life. They have no clue. Even a relationship/marriage therapist with no experience in cross-cultural life would not help much. If you are seeking one, then go for those who lived that life and helped many other interracial families.

Workplace Diversity

When you start your career in mixed cultures, it can be something completely new. It's quite a transition from your original work setup, where you were surrounded by your own community—people who spoke the same language and shared similar ethics and values.

In this new environment, you'll likely need to engage in small talk, demonstrate your value to climb the corporate ladder, and navigate numerous dinner gatherings and events. The range of communication skills required—whether in writing emails or presenting your ideas—can feel overwhelming at first. You might feel lost initially, but over time, you'll get the hang of it. Remember, you're not just learning; others are also learning from you. In these settings, you're not the only one growing—your colleagues are also gaining insights from your unique qualities and perspective. So, make sure to share your knowledge as they do with you. By teaching one another, you'll foster better relationships and create an excellent work environment. After all, that's the direction the world is heading—globally intertwined and interconnected. So, do your part.

As time passes, you'll adapt, but along the way, you'll make mistakes and face disappointments—and that's perfectly fine. Sometimes, the best way to learn is through failure and picking yourself back up. You might find yourself sitting among Germans for hours, not understanding a single word, remaining silent. You could ask them to speak in English, but instead, you stay quiet. Or you could challenge yourself to learn the language and beat them at their own game.

When people ask you for favors, like taking in a roommate, you may agree even if you don't want to. Don't do that. If your gut tells you no, listen to it. Sometimes, in the desire to be accepted or to fit in, you might prioritize pleasing others over your own needs and boundaries. Avoid that at all costs. People won't appreciate it or might even disrespect you, seeing you as unreliable. Eventually, they may begin to take advantage of you, expecting you to always say yes, even to things you dislike.

In groups of white people discussing aspects of your home country's culture, you might find yourself standing in silence, even when their words indirectly insult where you come from. They might criticize the way you eat, clean, or cook or make mockeries of the beliefs and values of your culture. Instead of speaking up and challenging their perspectives to help them understand, you stay quiet just to avoid being seen as the "bad guy."

In many situations, you'll be the only one receiving criticism about how things work in your home country, especially when comparing African and Western cultures. And yet, you say nothing. Don't. By staying silent, you're only encouraging disrespect and allowing ignorance to persist.

Maybe—just maybe—you are in that office or that job for a reason: to teach others and help them better understand the world. So, choose to speak up—enough with the silence. By holding everything in, you're not only harming your own well-being, but you're also failing to help them overcome their ignorance. Do your part.

Religion and Believes

When couples come from different religious backgrounds, it's important to address this early on. Discussing the values and beliefs that each person brings to the relationship is crucial. Differences in religion often involve holidays, ways of celebrating them, and decisions about where or whether to celebrate at all. For one partner, certain traditions might not be significant, while for the other, they could be deeply meaningful and a core part of their identity. In such relationships, conflicts may be inevitable.

You're a new couple, excited to celebrate one of the big holidays, like Christmas, together for the first time. Both you and your parents are thrilled. However, when you arrive, the food being served isn't to your partner's taste, and the prayers and ceremonies make him uncomfortable. He goes along with it, trying to make you happy, but he's eager for it all to be over and wants to leave as soon as possible. Meanwhile, you want to stay longer and enjoy time with your family. You notice he's becoming increasingly tense, and soon, you start to feel uncomfortable as well. So, you both decide to leave together. This leads to a conflict later that evening.

The next time Easter comes around, you visit to celebrate with the extended family in Europe. At the dinner table, everyone is speaking French. There's no prayer, fasting, or going to church—nothing that feels familiar. Hours pass, and you start feeling left out because no one speaks proper English, and even though some of them could, they refuse to. You're feeling bored, frustrated, and ready to leave. But if you do, it would be seen as rude and inconsiderate.

Now that you have children, certain religious ceremonies need to be performed shortly after birth, some within just a few days. As time passes, you may want to start teaching them about different worldviews—beliefs, rituals, values, and religious ceremonies. Then, when it's time for them to start school, these religious differences can impact decisions, including which school to choose. Subject choices become a point of contention, especially when it comes to whether they should study ethics or religion, but not both. The conflicting beliefs between you and your partner create confusion, leaving the children uncertain about what to believe. If you can't agree on giving them exposure to both perspectives, the children may feel torn, caught in the middle of trying to please both parents without knowing what to do.

To navigate these potential challenges, the couple should be open in communication about religion and beliefs during the dating phase—discuss viewpoints in a calm and harmonious way. Put clear things on the table. Include what matters the most to you and what things you can't compromise on. How certain things make you feel. And direct the discussion to bring you towards common understanding and acceptance. Make sure to respect your partner's beliefs, even if they sound funny, ridiculous, or unreal. When sensitive topics arise, know where to stop. It is important that you set boundaries where you stand and accept where your partner draws the boundary lines. Respect that and move on to the things you agree on, for example, being kind, loving, and treating humans well. The crucial thing to consider is that both your partner and you should not try to enforce each other's beliefs on each other. Forcing them to go to ceremonies and Sunday rituals can encourage resistance. If one of you has such interests, it is best to communicate directly so the other doesn't feel tricked into it.

Once you have established a family and children are involved, consider exposing them to both beliefs and values. One should not be discarded or devalued. Most conversations should strive to make compromises and find solutions that incorporate both perspectives. Until the children are old enough to decide for themselves, it's up to you, the parents, to allow them to navigate through the beliefs, the ceremonies, and the holidays as much as you can. Don't forget to be flexible and take things so seriously when mistakes happen. It's also possible to seek counseling or mediation if need be. The very most important thing to focus on here is the love and commitment you have for yourself and your family. Regardless of what miscommunications or conflicts might arise, it is important to remember the shared affection, what made you fall in love with each other, and most of all, what your responsibilities are for your children when you have kids.

Financial and Social Conflicts Management

Financial Conflicts

Financial conflict is common in most couples regardless of cultural or racial disparity—two things to consider here. When relationships are within mixed race, there is assumed income disparity and actual income disparity. Both affect the couple in different ways. Assumed inequality due to the county of origin. One from a wealthy country and the other from a developing country. Even though the person earns well, there is this assumption that by oneself, your partner, or others, you are unequal. Creating anxiety and discomfort between the couple when topics of finances arise. The second one is where one partner earns better than the other one. In such a scenario, the one who earns better feels financially burdened, while the other feels anxious and desperate to contribute to the relationship—putting both under pressure and bringing uncomfortable conversation. At times, it brings power imbalance and insecurity. Which in turn can lead to resentment and breakups if not handled well.

To avoid this and minimize conflicts, there are a couple of things you can do. Decide to work together through open communication. Include your feelings, financial goals, plans, and things you want to invest in. One might prefer traveling more than buying a house. One might prefer having a low-level car and buying a better house. One might find having a good car than settling somewhere. Choices between where to invest in housing or business need to be transparent. Discussing in clear terms finds a middle ground to establish financial boundaries and respect income differences. Focus on finding an effective approach that can bring you to agreement on budgets and future plans. Most importantly, it is important to know that, as with many other sacrifices we make in our relationships, there are certain things you need to compromise to work this out. Remember, living in harmony with clear understanding and minimizing conflict is the aim here. While you are at it, prioritize open communication, respect one another's financial status, set clear financial goals together, and address issues with a sense of unity as they occur.

Social Conflicts: Navigating Family Dynamics and Preventing Disputes

Undoubtfully, Family dynamics can be complex. One looks down on the other's race. The other feels superior to the other. One feels less of the other because of economic reasons. The other feels entitled because of the color of the skin. At times, one race is seen as a potential criminal when something goes missing. One speaks loudly, while the other assumes being loud is disrespectful and not a way of showing importance. One says don't come to my house unannounced while visits are a genuine way of showing that the person cares. Each side is competing to prove who is right without recognizing the importance of the collective well-being of the family. Varied viewpoints and misinterpretations raise tension within the family.

In mixed couples, family values shaped by unique cultures and experiences make it challenging. Besides knowing how to communicate you would need a lot of emotional strength to go through some conflicting situations. Discussions can be affected by ego and varying personalities. Addressing issues, especially sensitive issues, is difficult. Mixed couple families come from personalities and values molded by multiple experiences. To navigate this family dynamic will require you open communication and active listening. Communicating with the intent of clarifying and not undervaluing the other's values, listening without judgment, and pure intent to understand.

Preventing conflict requires developing those communication skills, and those conversations should lead to solving matters constructively. The people involved will need to meet halfway. Adopting the mindset of 'I might be wrong, let me listen to their perspective' can be helpful. This way, conflicts can be resolved with flexibility, acceptance, and understanding of differences. This helps prevent future conflicts and preserves the stability of the family dynamic.

Healthy Leaning In

Embracing Differences: Building Connection and Common Ground in Cross-Cultural Relationships

You find yourself in a world where you need to be constantly careful not to displease anyone. Eventually, this creates a sense of discomfort and a negative attitude because it pressures you to hide your true self. Compromising on your internal comfort to make others comfortable. Which is not healthy. How about you try grace instead?

You see, at every social gathering, conversations often shift to topics that make you uncomfortable. You feel uneasy, even though you're there to enjoy the evening or a simple lunch. As time goes on, when you think you've got everything figured out and things are finally going well, you end up caught in the same cycle of social events with people from different backgrounds. They continue to say the same negative things about your culture, things that don't align with who you truly are.

Such repeated experiences can chip away at your self-worth, make you doubt yourself, and erode your confidence if you let them. You might feel undervalued at work, passing up leadership opportunities to others with less experience. You could start internalizing stereotypes, like believing African women aren't seen as capable of such responsibilities and are viewed merely as dating material. You might even begin to think of yourself as a "bad driver" because you're Chinese or accept the idea that, as a German, you're heartless—and over time, you could start acting that way. Don't let those stereotypes define you. Break free from that mindset immediately. Recognize that their view is just that—their perspective, not your reality. In that moment, let your own reality take charge, not their lens. Be unapologetically yourself—imperfect, yes, but uniquely and authentically you. Walk with your head held high, embracing the good person you are. What you allow into your mind shapes your thoughts. Your thoughts shape your actions, and your actions create the reality in which you live. So, take charge of that reality.

Shape it based on what you truly believe in and the unity you're working to build. This won't stop, but your perspective on life is changed now. You want unity to triumph over division. You want love to conquer hate. You choose to show grace to yourself and extend that grace to others. You educate because, sometimes, people genuinely don't know and are caught in their own ignorance, not having experienced the world the way you do. And that's okay.

That's when you start to realize how others' misconceptions about you and your cultural background have been shaping your experiences all along. It becomes clear that speaking up is crucial, and understanding the reasons behind people's assumptions and actions is key. You begin asking questions one by one, gradually sharing your truths while staying authentic. You embrace and accept who you are. Educating those unfamiliar with your culture and learning about others helps you grow step by step. Lean into learning rather than making assumptions on your journey through life as you navigate it alongside those around you. This is the intentional, healthy growth you've needed all along.

Now, whenever a new person joins the group or you meet someone new, take a moment to understand their perspective before responding. Regardless of whether their experiences have been positive or negative, focus on listening and learning. This approach helps build meaningful relationships grounded in an appreciation for the world's diversity and sincere respect for its beautiful differences, free from judgment or condescension.

In simple terms, if your first instinct is to reject your differences and focus solely on your similarities, you'll hinder your growth and learning as an individual, a couple, or a family. Allow life to teach you. Approach experiences as an observer, not as someone being targeted. Don't dwell on issues from days or even hours ago. Instead, address the situation directly and make the choice to let it go.

Holding onto these feelings can intensify their effect on your soul. Protect your peace. Set boundaries to close off openings that allow negativity to enter and safeguard your joy in life. Only when your mind and soul are at peace can you have a full cup to pour love into your relationships and home. The next time something similar happens, it can trigger past emotions, creating a buildup over time. You might start avoiding these conversations and build walls to shield yourself from further hurt. This can impact your communication and lead to resentment. At that point, healing becomes more difficult, and you may need therapy to repair those damaged connections.

Before it's too late, be open to learning. Have those uncomfortable conversations when you're calm, and cultivate the ability to let go of the differences between you. As humans, we often focus on what we dislike or what sets us apart. But if we took the time to recognize the commonalities we share and the things we agree on, we could build stronger relationships and create more meaningful moments together. Let's be among those who choose to learn from each other rather than reject one another.

Understanding and managing these areas will help you build stronger relationships and navigate challenges with greater clarity. Avoid focusing on the negatives and the potential impacts you assume they'll have on you, your children, and your loved ones. Instead, lean into learning and teaching. Embrace the healthy, joyful aspects of life. By acknowledging conflicts, finding common ground, and celebrating your differences, you'll strengthen your bond more than ever.

The Mission Is Beyond You

Ultimately, it's important to understand that your union has a greater purpose. If you take nothing else from this book, remember this: your unity together serves a higher mission, and you are entrusted with fulfilling it. However, to succeed, you must recognize that the darker forces in this world will try to resist your success because your union has the power to create significant unity and bring about change. See your impact in the bigger picture. You were born for a purpose in your unique ways, and with your unique experiences, you're to build something unique that requires that uniqueness. Remind yourself that each morning, you wake up to a new day because you have a mission to fulfill—whether it's your work, studies, serving others, raising your children, or supporting your partner. Be mindful of the vulnerabilities that could allow adversaries to undermine what you've built, shake your true essence, and disrupt your relationships.

Like most people, you seek to understand the purpose of your life on this earth—whether through your work, raising children, or using your talents and skills. You have a deep desire to serve communities and humanity, whether on a small scale or a larger one. This purpose can manifest in many ways: nurturing a future champion as a parent, being a preacher, a leader, a podcast host, an artist, working with refugees, or healing others as a psychiatrist: every conversation and social encounter matters. So, make it count. Make your existence on this planet meaningful and impactful for good.

Remember, pursuing these purposes often involves tests and challenges that foster personal growth. The trials you face in your relationship and life aren't just for your development—they serve a higher purpose that impacts future generations. So, when times get tough, revisit the insights you've recorded or reflected on to remind yourself of the bigger picture.

The same applies to cross-country agreements, intercultural business partnerships, friendships, and beyond. Whenever someone from a different country crosses your path, embrace the opportunity to learn. Appreciate how the universe guides you to new places and teaches you through both good and challenging experiences. Most importantly, approach it wisely—use the guidance in this book to save time and energy and avoid unnecessary disappointments.

Core Lesson

Life feels lighter when you lean into challenges with balance and remember the mission is bigger than you.

ABOUT THE AUTHOR

Seble Lemma Dessalegne is a cross-cultural health and fitness coach, digital health advocate, and founder of Bond Beyond Borders. With over a decade of experience across Africa, Europe, Asia, and the United States, she combines professional expertise with personal insight into the challenges of identity, belonging, and communication in a multicultural world.

Having lived and worked in diverse cultural settings, she understands the joys and challenges of creating meaningful connections across borders. Passionate about guiding individuals, families, and organizations, she helps people navigate cultural differences, strengthen relationships, and build resilience.

With a background in international relations and a career spanning healthcare, wellness, and health innovation, her work sits at the intersection of people, technology, and culture. Through her company *Tenachin*—meaning "our health" in Amharic—she develops programs that brings together culture, wellness, and innovation to support communities

As a mother raising children in a multicultural family, Seble understands the balance between heritage, identity, and global living. Her human-centered approach—shaped by personal experience, coaching, and global travel—empowers readers to navigate differences with confidence, strengthen relationships, and thrive in all aspects of life..

www.ingramcontent.com/pod-product-compliance
Lightning Source LLC
Chambersburg PA
CBHW020535030426
42337CB00013B/860